MW00439848

Big
Bold
Beautiful

A Memoir of Self-Esteem

Jennifer S. Kim

Copyright © 2019 Jennifer S. Kim

All rights reserved

ISBN: 9781703707793

Edited by Jeff Karon and Sarah Yuen
Photo Credits: Sunny Shih

Author's Note

This memoir is the complete opposite of how I once viewed myself: small, timid, and ugly. Period.

I never thought I could write a book. Many people have encouraged me to write one about the suffering I endured as a young child. I often hesitated, but I finally plucked up the courage!

I have never read avidly nor been verbally expressive so writing this memoir was not easy. However, it became a major battlefield due to my epilepsy. Reduced cognition from years of illness created a significant barrier to creative writing. But thanks to my editors, I can now frankly share the story of my life.

This memoir feels like a short autobiography, but it's really just a taste of the interrelated trials I have faced in my life - each stage being a stepping stone to the next.

Thank you so much to my dear friends for your honest critique and advice. Vicky Hyun deserves much thanks for helping me complete the book. Dr. Robyn Kassas, founder of TORCC NYC, you played an instrumental role in encouraging me to share my life story with others. I could not have done it without your wise words.

Dedication

This book is dedicated to all those who have gone through similar circumstances of social opposition and family dysfunction that has lead to issues of low confidence and self-esteem. Judgment and negative words inflict wounds so deeply in us that it can take years to heal them.

I stand in solidarity with all, extending as much compassion as I can offer.

This book contains my personal story. I write my story as it is. Photos are available in this book. What I share in this book is not intended to be construed as medical advice. Some names, locations, and identifying characteristics have been changed to protect the privacy of those depicted.

Contents

Chapter 1
Like a Prologue

"How would you like your hair done today? A French braid or a half braid?" my mom would ask.

"I choose a half braid," I would shout back happily.

I was a happy, vibrant child, who loved her parents and loved her hair. My mom took great pains to make it look as pretty as possible, so I would stand out among all the other little girls in New York City.

I liked to stand out. I loved to sing and dance and act and be different.

But that was then.

We lived in a small apartment building in the Bronx. Everyday my parents, with me in an old-fashioned brown car with a super long trunk, would drive to a little store my dad ran there.

We had a security guard who kept everything safe all day. The Bronx in the 1990s was a scary place, but I didn't see it. I was four-years-old and that shop was my stage.

I staved off boredom while my parents worked by, grabbing my red and white toy microphone and joyfully singing my favorite songs, while dancing for anyone who happened by the store. I loved the way people smiled at me, even though they didn't understand the Korean lyrics.

I sang at home too. I sang whenever an opportunity presented itself.

My parents were very proud of my voice and never interrupted me, or asked me to be quiet, no matter how loudly I sang.

Once, an African-American lady walked past the store with her little daughter, who appeared to be the same age as me. When she saw me performing she hollered,

"Woah, look at this Asian girl. She's got the moves and can sing it out! Don't be shy! You can too! Dance it out. You gotta do it just like her; okay?"

I was usually shy around African-Americans who lived all around the store. They often teased me. They would try to imitate me and shout mocking words that sounded like Chinese, but weren't. Now this little girl turned her head to look at me with admiration. It was a new feeling for me.

So proud of her mother's words, I asked my mom to teach me even more Korean songs.

When my mom was not helping my dad, she would spend free time taking many pictures of me; before I was five-years-old she must have taken literally hundreds of pictures of me. I would wear a beautiful dress and pose like a model in our backyard, with my hands on my hips or lying down with my arms folded behind my head.

Other times, my mom would take me sightseeing in the city, and then she would take pictures of me at the Museum of Modern Art, Central Park, Rockefeller Center, and the Statue of Liberty.

My mom was a faithful believer for many years, so when she spoke about God, I too believed. At dinnertime, she would take pictures of me praying before I ate at my own small table, or lifting my hands to worship God. There were times when she would take photos of me reading a children's Bible storybook on my own. All around me there was poverty, crime, and neglect but I was treasured.

The Bronx may have been a disadvantaged borough in New York City but it was rich in musical and artistic talent. I was in awe of the graffiti as I walked each block, past each apartment building.

I used to marvel equally at the afro hairstyles sported by the young black men. I thought their hair was amazing, but my mom told me that hairstyle was indicative of gang membership.

My dad was a very law-abiding man but he had to buy products to sell in his store which would be bought by the gang members and other local criminals. If he didn't, his business would easily shut down. Every other week, my dad and I would drive to Manhattan for new stock. I was joyful he allowed me to go with him to watch what he would shop for. If not, I would continue to stay bored in the store all day.

Along with the toys, handkerchiefs, and hats, he would buy pocket knives, firecrackers, wigs, and afro hair products. It was not just a routine trip. It was not uncommon for my dad's car to be robbed on the way home, so he never purchased too much merchandise at once. Thankfully it never happened when I was with him. I was never allowed to be left alone in the car or I could have been kidnapped and have every single object robbed in his car.

My dad did what was necessary to survive and provide for us.

Unfortunately, pocketknives were often sold out in Manhattan. When they didn't have any, I would watch my dad sigh in frustration and dash out of the store. He would speed from Manhattan to Brooklyn and eventually to Staten

Island, where he was confident he could find knives of superior quality. Pocketknives were in great demand in the 90's New York.

Where Did It Start?

I believe I inherited my innate self-confidence from my dad. He was a risk-taker, and I was so proud of him.

One day, a young girl came into the store to buy illegal firecrackers. Of course I didn't know they were illegal at the time. I just saw her being approached by a policeman as she left our store. He was asking her questions. She was told that if she refused to confess where she had bought them, her parents would be put to jail. As a result, the girl walked back to the store, and led the policeman over to my dad.

"He's the one who sold them to me!" I heard her shout.

The policeman handcuffed my dad and took him away. My mom sobbed and ran after my dad as he was being put into the police car. I waited for him to reassure her, and tell her and me, everything would be okay. Instead he turned to her and declared in Korean,

"Make sure you sell all the remaining firecrackers by tonight!"

They kept him in jail overnight. I knew he must have been so brave. He was my hero.

I never considered my dad a scary or stern father. He spoiled me and gave me whatever I wanted. Once at a toy store, I was admiring a colorful bicycle with training wheels. When my dad had finished paying for his merchandise, he walked away from the cashier.

"Jenn, let's leave now," he said.

I did not budge; I just stared at the bike. When he noticed I wasn't beside him, he turned around, then chuckled and asked the owner how much the bike cost.

The twenty-five-dollar price tag was high, but I beamed as I walked out with a brand new bicycle with bright blue and pink wheels. I loved receiving gifts but quality time with my parents was my number one love language as a little one.

Driving on the highway one sunny day, I stared at my dad intently for a long moment thinking,

I wonder why my dad, unlike my mom, is so quiet. I wonder why he doesn't talk to me— but it's okay. He loves me because he likes to be with me and lets me follow him to shop in the city.

Although I was loved by both my parents, the connection with my dad seemed more special. I secretly loved my dad more than I did my mom.

Just before I turned five, my family moved to Flushing, in the borough of Queens. I was old enough now to enter kindergarten, and my parents wanted to place me in a public school which would offer a good education. They were also concerned about my safety outside of the school. Flushing was clean and quiet, and certainly not as busy as the Bronx. There were different ethnic groups and a larger number of Asians in Flushing. There were hardly any Asians in the Bronx.

Shortly after the move, my mom and my aunt took me to a store with large mirrors and big seats. After we walked in, a lady stood in front of me, smiling enthusiastically, and placed me in a small chair. She washed my hair and then trimmed it, then she applied cotton balls all over my head, tucking them behind my ears while pouring liquid onto my head. I had no idea what she was doing to my shoulder length silky black hair, but I trusted my mom enough to just fall asleep. I shouldn't have done that.

An hour later when I woke up, the lady was removing the rolls, and then she rewashed and blew dry my hair. I looked at myself in the mirror in horror— she had given me a perm!

I cried all the way home while my mom carried me on her back. I was so embarrassed by these new curls. I was angry at my mom for not telling me this. When visitors came over to our house I was sullen and withdrawn. My hair, which I had loved so much, had been replaced by a frizzy mess. At least it grew out. But my hair was very important to my self-worth and when it was a mess, I was a mess too.

My First Perm, 1993

A few months before kindergarten began, my parents sent me to a Korean nursery school. It was my first time I had seen a flood of children running around in one place. My heart was beating and was about to break into tears until I noticed a girl in a pink dress sitting in the middle of the room sobbing. I slowly walked up to her.

"Why are you crying?" I asked, softly touching her arm.

"Everyone's making fun of me because I'm smaller than them," she told me.

Crystal and I became good friends. She was the shortest of the 100 children in the nursery school. I was only three inches taller, yet I was the average height for the girls in the class. When we were small, height was everything.

What Pride Led To

John was another child the kids laughed at. He was bald. No one knew why. He just was. Because all the kids made fun of him, I did too. We labeled him, *"The Boy with the Lion King Cap."*

Every month when students had birthdays, the teachers called forward in turn one child of the opposite sex to kiss each birthday boy or girl on the cheeks; a common practice in most Korean nursery schools. My birthday was in July, and when the time came I stood in the middle of the line in the gym, waiting for someone to kiss me. The teacher asked all the boys,

"Now who wants to kiss Jennifer for her birthday?"

There was no answer.

I secretly had a crush on a boy named Daniel but he could not kiss me because his birthday was the same month as mine and he was standing right behind me in line. When a girl I disliked volunteered to kiss him instead, I envied her with the heat of a thousand suns.

I told myself I didn't want anyone to kiss me anyway since they had taken their turns earlier in the year, and I certainly didn't want John, the bald boy, to kiss me. Suddenly, I heard the teacher shout,

"John, can you come and kiss Jenn?"

He walked slowly up to me and kissed me on the cheeks. I grimaced, embarrassed, reviled by his oddness. I feared being judged by the other students since then.

I was a prideful child. I can remember what I said to myself in front of my parent's store one day, *My hair is beautiful. I can sing. I am tall, my parents love me, and my life is perfect, so I think I am God.* After much thought and deliberation, I concluded, *No, I am God!*

One year later, I was diagnosed with brain cancer.

Chapter 2
A Life Turned Upside Down

During first grade, at the afterschool program that I was attending, the teachers announced that students could go trick-or-treating on Halloween. This would be my first time going trick-or-treating. Four of my friends and I decided to go together, and when the day came I was so excited.

On Halloween, as I walked back to class after lunch in school, all I could think of was my brand new blue dress with real lace which my mom had bought me the night before.

"Jenn, do you like this one?" My mom gingerly pulled the dress out of a cupboard.

I had nodded and smiled enthusiastically shouting, "Yes!"

By 12:40 p.m., I could not concentrate on Mrs. Chin's lesson on the Pilgrims. I thought knocking on doors for candies would never come.

Suddenly, there was a knock on the classroom door. Mrs. Chin opened it, and there stood my dad. He wanted to take me out of the class. I gladly ran out and jumped into his arms and then our car.

My dad rushed me into his brown car. He drove me into the suburbs where there were no stores or restaurants. Instead we only saw bizarre, tree-lined streets. I thought this was odd, and I wondered why my dad had picked me up. But I did not care to ask as I was happy to be out of class. I only hoped he would take me back in time for trick-or-treating.

We arrived at a big building with a quiet lobby. A lady asked us to sit and wait. I did not know it was a hospital— North Shore University Hospital. I thought it was a corporation my dad was visiting for work purposes. Someone brought my dad a lot of papers to sign and we waited some more until 4 p.m. A woman dressed in green then brought me to a room where I was given a gown to wear.

I realized she was a nurse. I immediately began to rebel and whine, yelling at the nurse. I asked why I had to wear the gown. When she didn't answer I grew even more angry. After ten minutes or so, my dad, who had heard my yelling, walked into the room.

"Dad, why does she want me to wear this? I'm not sick! And I have to go trick-or-treating today!"

"I know, but you must wear this gown."

"I don't want to. Why didn't you tell me about this?"

"Because you are sick and the doctors want you to have an operation immediately," he said, not once raising his voice.

I was shocked.

"What? No, I'm healthy," I sobbed.

My dad got on his knees, let out a deep sigh, and said,

"Jenn, you know it yourself, right? Suddenly getting car-sick daily, vomiting every night after dinner, waking up with scary dreams about death. This has been happening for a whole year. You are a big girl now. Don't be a liar. You know you are sick, right?"

I knew he was right but I was in denial and refused to admit this. After a long silence, I nodded.

"But what about trick-or-treating? I have to go."

"If you go tonight, you might die tomorrow. Then I will never see you again. So Jenn, will you please wear this gown," my dad insisted, rather morbidly.

After wrestling with the decision for a few moments, I reluctantly grabbed the gown. I walked into the operating room, changed into the gown, and lay down on the surgical bed. After counting 100 sheep backward, I drifted off. It was a six-hour-long operation. The night of Halloween was my last day of first grade.

* * * * * * * * * * *

Opening my eyes slowly, I woke up abruptly remembering where I was. The first thing I spotted was the clock on the blue wall, its arms pointing to nearly 12 a.m. Turning my head to the right, I glanced at my reflection in the window and saw that my entire head was wrapped in a white bandage. The right half of my head was flat. It looked as if it had been sliced off. I was about to burst into tears when I heard a knock on the door.

The same nurse who had asked me to put on the gown entered. She grabbed a clean, white pillowcase, cut two almond-shaped holes near its base, and dressed me up as a ghost. Taking me out of the room, she carried me to each room and ward in the hallway, shouting,

"Trick-or-treat!"

A week after I was discharged, my dad and I made routine trips to the hospital for me to receive radiation and chemotherapy every week for the next six months. Listening to the loud sound in the room for thirty minutes on each of these mornings was annoying, but I did not have a choice. After the sessions ended, my dad drove me back home and went straight to work. I stayed alone in our house from 11 a.m. until my parents returned from work at 6 p.m. I was six-years-old.

After the chemotherapy and radiation treatment ended, the doctors required me to stay home and recuperate for the entire rest of the school year. It was thought that doing too much would exhaust my immune system and allow the cancer to return. My parents could not afford to pay a babysitter. The medical bills were rising and their business was slowing down, so I stayed home alone. With no television or toys to play with to keep me company, all I could do all day was watch my hair follicles fall out of my whole body; my waist growing thinner and thinner, and my skin color changing.

* * * * * * * * * *

My whole life had changed. This year was marked by loneliness and solitude. I could not wait until my friends came home from school. I ran out to play with them until my parents came home. During the summer, I spent a lot of time playing with my next-door neighbor, Aisha.

I was so excited at the approach of the new school year but I had missed almost all of first grade. I was told I had to repeat it, while all my friends went into the second grade. I whined for a while, feeling ashamed I will be judged by all students in school. In time, my parents requested the school board to accommodate me, and they told me the school officials would permit me to enter second grade if I learned to read before school started.

So, during the summer, I was homeschooled each morning by a teacher who taught me phonics well enough so I was able to enter the appropriate grade. I was satisfied that I was not held back because I didn't want to be undermined by students including adults.

All of the hair I had lost from head to toe gradually grew back, except for a large portion of my scalp that remained permanently bald. The treatment to kill the remaining cancer cells had also killed my hair cells, causing my hair follicles to die.

I remember my mom telling me on the first day of school,

"Jenn, when kids make fun of you for wearing a hat to school, don't feel upset or hurt by what they say."

When she said it, I could not comprehend what she meant. I did not understand why she thought they would tease me. The friends I had been playing with all year had not made fun of me. But of course, she knew better. I suppose I had forgotten about John and how we had treated him. I was just so excited to get back to school. I would not have been if I had known what was to come. So I paid no close attention to that advice.

But it started straight away.

When students of all grades waited in the cafeteria before heading to class in the morning, an African-American girl and I had an argument. We were in the same grade. Suddenly she asked me,

"Why do you always wear that hat?"

"I don't know" I said. I was too humiliated to tell.

"You always wear that."

"Because I want to!" I shouted. It was repeated over and over again.

The girl shouted something I could not hear because the cafeteria was so loud. Without care, I shouted back, "Fine!" Then she walked over to the other side of the table where we were sitting and snatched it off. The entire student body stared at me in shock, with their eyes wide open. She was the first person to take it off. Unable to handle the situation, I started crying. One of the school aides intervened and sent the girl to stand by the wall for misbehavior.

As I passed by her to walk to class, I supposed she wanted a solid answer before taking it off out of curiosity. But the damage was done.

Instead of looking down on her as I walked past to head to class, I gave her a look of shame as she returned an evil smile.

Students then began asking the same question while I responded to the same answer nervously all the time.

"Why do you always wear that hat?"

"Because I want to!"

* * * * * * * * *

One evening, I watched a Korean documentary about a girl my age who was suffering from leukemia. I related to her immensely because she could not attend school, had no friends, and was treated as inferior by her peers. She was suffering greatly. After the film ended I was reflecting deeply about it. I slowly walked up to my mom to find an answer.

"Mom, why did I get brain cancer?"

She was cooking Korean stew and was caught off guard. After a long time, she sighed heavily.

"I don't know what caused it. There are many things that can cause cancer Jenn. But I can't thank your pediatrician Dr. Jung enough for catching the sign of cancer. And one thing is for sure…it's a miracle you are alive…"

She proceeded to show me a piece of tofu using her ladle— white and soft.

"You see this? This is what the surgeons at the hospital had shown us; what it looked like. You should be happy that the tumor wasn't any bigger than the size of a quarter, or you would have died. So, thank Jesus, you are alive!"

Jesus? He saved my life? I asked myself as I slowly walked away. I was relieved after hearing my mom's encouraging words. I was in reverent awe of the way that He saved me through my pediatrician. I knew that if Jesus healed me, He could certainly help others too; maybe even the girl in the documentary.

That night for the first time before going to sleep I kneeled in bed and prayed.

"Thank you, Jesus, for saving my life. Without you, I would not be alive. I love you so much!"

I joyfully went to sleep after the prayer. I began to value myself and build resilience. I was so touched to know I was a survivor that I had quickly forgotten about the moments that I was embarrassed about my appearance. I did not find wearing my blue hat to be a burden. All I cared about was that someone who loved me had saved me.

BIG BOLD BEAUTIFUL

Chapter 3
Where Taunting Led

Unfortunately, my new-found self-assurance quickly vanished. I was suddenly assailed by insecurity and distrust of others as I started the third grade. The boys began calling me "*Baldy*". They were mostly Korean boys. During lunchtime, they would grab my hat and point at my head, laughing at my bald spot. This became a habit as they took turns to do this.

When I forgot to say, "excuse me" to a student, he would say nothing but take off my hat. I tried to play tag with some friends but stopped out of fear that a boy might grab my hat while I was running around. I never talked or fought back—all I did was cry.

Crying became a touchstone in my life. Looking back, I realize I used *crying* to create a barrier between the boys and myself. Whenever I started crying, the school aide would remove the boys and make them stand against a lunch wall or sit in a corner, so it was my power over them. But I was still afraid of them. It would have helped greatly if they were told to apologize and promise never to do it again. But this never happened. Instead, I cultivated and survived on pity, and not just from the children.

One day, I was swimming in the pool at a Korean summer school at the end of third grade. A male teacher unexpectedly removed my hat, took one quick glance, and then put it back on while continuing to swim with the young boys. I sobbed at the look on his face and those of the boys.

17

The female teachers came to console me, and I realized that he had just wanted to know what my head looked like, out of curiosity. He came back simply to make an apology, but I refused to accept it and avoided him.

I became increasingly sensitive towards males, young or old, during my childhood. I began to consider myself abnormal. It grew even worse in the fourth grade.

Doctors had noted that the cancer treatment might cause long-term effects of anxiety and depression. Having cancer, enduring the treatments necessary and always being afraid it might come back made me anxious. My anxiety became acute at the beginning of fourth grade. My hands would shake fiercely whenever I had to practice writing, making me embarrassed and distressed. I already found it difficult to write because I was left-handed. My hands shook in class and whenever I did my homework. It scared me how much they shook, so I kept it a secret from my parents and friends. I was terrified the girls might find out. To hide my envy at the good penmanship of many girls, I secretly copied their writing styles.

I was remarkably self-conscious of the boys' typical approach. Whenever they were around, I avoided eye contact and bowed my head so they wouldn't see my face flush. If I was talking to a friend and a boy walked pass I went silent and prayed they wouldn't hear the pounding of my racing heart.

Outside of School

One day, Laura, a close friend of mine, invited me to a Korean Christian church service. She enjoyed attending them and noticed there were a great number of children around our age. At first, I gave an immediate "no," preferring to avoid meeting new people in case they judged me. But after her constant pleading, I agreed to make a visit. Since I had no friends other than Crystal and Laura, I took a chance to look for companionship—to make at least one more friend who would accept me as a normal, not weird one. I hoped that if I was introduced as her friend, the members might look upon me kindly.

The church was enormous. The stairs up to the chapel seemed to go on forever and completely wore me out. The service was short and meaningful. I enjoyed the contemporary children's worship songs and the Bible message by the children's pastor. After hearing the pastor's message to the young children and seeing children who attended the same primary school as me gave me a longing to attend the church. This was so I can learn more from the message, joyfully praise songs, and bond closer with children in church.

As a newcomer, I was introduced to the entire congregation. A Sunday School teacher held my hand and walked me down the long, narrow aisle as music played, as if I were getting married. It was mortifying. The girls from my school, especially the first-grade young girls whispered to each other, glaring. I heard one say to the other with every step I took,

"Why does she always wear that hat?"

"Yeah, I always see her wearing that!"

"Why do you always wear that hat?" they asked.

Suddenly, a child in the back shouted,

"Hey, that's *The Girl with the Hat!*"

I braced for the over-analyzing to commence, but a boy, James, who was also from my school shouted back,

"No, her name is *Jennifer,* not *'The Girl with the Hat!'*"

Despite his support my emotions overwhelmed me. Itching to leave the seat as soon as the service ended, I rushed outside with tears rolling down my cheeks. The Sunday School teachers tried to stop me, asking me to stay behind for activities and snacks, and so did Laura. They attempted to calm me down while listening to my pain, but I could not. I needed to go home and hide.

I had never felt so emotionally wounded by such a large crowd. After this experience, whenever I encountered peers from church, school, park, or the neighborhood, I knew they were all saying behind my back,

"That's *The Girl with the Hat.*"

Even some of the shy girls had become comfortable calling me this. Mischievous boys called me "*Baldy*" seizing every chance they had, and "*Cry Baby*" for crying so frequently. From this, I conceptualized that it would be hard to "fit in" with anyone.

I became even more isolated, staying home to avoid the mocking. All I could do was watch television to lose the risk of listening to even a single taunt and dodge anyone trying to take off my hat. I held onto my hat tightly whenever I left the house. It was difficult to cope— the thought of gluing my hat to my head would have been less agonizing.

Chapter 4
Her Verbal Abuse

The constant rejection and ridicule by the kids began to be echoed at home. When I turned nine, my parents started verbally and physically abusing me.

With the trauma of my brain cancer, combined with this new abuse, my anxiety increased.

I knew it hadn't been easy for my parents. After the discovery of my brain tumor, my parents were under a lot of pressure. The diagnosis, the medical debts, and the loss of their business all at once, weighed heavily on them.

The birth of my little sister, Eunice, added to their troubles, and did little to cement a faltering relationship. I knew they had been considering divorce before I was sick, but they decided to stay together to support me. If I had not contracted cancer, I do not know what would have happened to my family.

Traditional Korean culture set no clear boundaries on emotional and physical discipline. Hitting, slapping, or fiercely scolding a child as a lesson was widely accepted during my parents' childhood. Parents, teachers, and other elders in the community were expected to enforce this kind of discipline on young ones. Usually, it was done lovingly and was not meant to be abusive. But as my parents' marriage deteriorated, our home life became very unstable.

It was impossible to predict when something or someone would set my parents off. I was never sure what would displease them, especially to my mom. She was obsessed with perfection and her unrealistic expectations took a huge toll on me. When I did not meet the strictest of requirements in either my chores or the other responsibilities assigned to me, she would complain nonstop about me for the rest of the day.

My mom never spoke serenely. When she wanted a chore done, she would yell at me, instead of asking me in a calm voice. When I was vacuuming, my mom paid exceedingly close attention to what I was doing, looking for every single piece of dirt or dust I might have missed. When she found some, she would yell,

"No, no, no, no! You have to vacuum every corner in the room! Why didn't you listen to what I said? No, Jenn! Vacuum all the spaces underneath the bed mattress!"

My heart would quake at her tone. It was so different from the mommy I had grown up with to that point. It was as though all that love and affection, and pride, had vanished. I grieved for that and endured even more ridicule because she did not give me any specific instructions in advance. If I had known exactly what she wanted me to do, I would have diligently followed her directions and performed the chores more successfully.

Organizing everything in the house was also excessively important to my mom. Making my bed with the blanket evenly laid out each morning was crucial to her. I would suffer the wrath of a thousand suns if I so much as slightly delayed in doing this. If she asked me to fold the clothes and towels after the laundry was dry, it was like working with origami paper.

Firstly, I had to make sure there were no wrinkles. Next, I had to fold the towels exactly in half and carefully lay them on top of each other—not lopsided, but perfectly aligned.

If I did not complete this ritual correctly, I was viciously chastised for not being careful enough. Considering that she never seemed pleased when she assessed my work, I had to endure her constant nagging and correcting, no matter how good a job I had done.

"Hurry up! Why do you have to be so slow?"

If I did not come into the living room within ten seconds of her calling us for dinner, my mom would yell from the end of the room.

It never occurred to her to allow me the time for me to finish reading the last page of a chapter from a book, or give my last say to someone on the phone. When I tried to defend myself, she would simply shout,

"Be quiet!"

I would take my place at the table and lift my chopsticks with jittery hands.

Then it was time to learn how to cook. My mom showed me how to cut, peel, and slice fruits and vegetables. One day after dinner, I peeled and sliced a Fuji apple—one of my dad's favorite fruits—to share with him. When I did not slice the apple the way my mom had taught me, she came into my bedroom later and complained,

"Why didn't you slice the apple like I said? Slice it nicely, or it won't look pretty."

A week later, I tried to cut and slice an apple more precisely. I was yearning to hear some sort of praise from my mom, but I failed to please her again. After dinner, she came into my room and grumbled in an even harsher tone.

"I reminded you to slice the apples nicely, which you did okay today, but why didn't you peel all of the skin off of the apple? Remember, I taught you that you must slice it nicely so it looks enticing!"

As she slammed the door shut, I curled up into a ball and sobbed, frozen by her harsh words. After that, whenever I was doing tasks while my mom was around, my heart would pound, and my nervousness would cause me to be clumsy or make even more mistakes. It was difficult to endure the pain and suffering of her negative words that made me feel so worthless.

At dinner one night, my mom asked me to bring bowls of Kimchi stew from the stove to the dinner table. I tried my best to bring them without spilling a single drop.

But my hands would not stop shaking, and I ended up spilling not a drop but a puddle of the stew onto the dinner table. I knew what was coming. After enduring my mom's screams, I beat myself up for the rest of the night. Her frequent, humiliating comments brainwashed me into further internalizing the belief that I could do nothing perfectly. I told myself I was worthless, a girl with no value, and I felt extremely intimidated even by my own family.

Since my parents, particularly my mom, never gave me a chance to prove my worth, I was disheartened. It was hard for her to take perspective of my thoughts and actions. When I tried even a little bit to defend myself, the first thing I would hear was,

"Be quiet! How dare you talk back to adults!"

She continued to scold me for my "offensive" and "audacious" actions, and for giving my own opinion. To convince herself that she was always right, her response, words of excuse would always start with,

"You know why?"

Eventually, my mom's deep persuasion forced me to believe she was always right and I was always in the wrong. So sensitive to random people's words, I would weep directly in their faces when they tried to give me even a simple advice because I was absolutely convinced I could not do anything well. It was so hard to handle even the smallest criticism from anyone. My weeping created great stress to many teachers, at which point they often avoided me or became reluctant to assist me.

BIG BOLD BEAUTIFUL

Chapter 5
No Longer Daddy's Girl

My dad took the abuse to another level. Whenever I refused to do something he had asked me to do, he instantly smacked me on the right side of my head; always on my bald spot. Being hit there was particularly upsetting, since the bald spot caused me not only physical pain but also the fear that he might cause lasting damage. It also felt like my dad was lashing out at the part of me which was deficient. I took this abuse personally as a young child.

One night, I argued with my dad after refusing to visit my aunt's house, because I was frightened by her. She always looked so unwelcoming.

"We will be going to your aunt's house tonight," he said.

"I don't want to, I'll just stay home," I said.

"Let's just go," he insisted.

"No, I don't want to. She's too scary," I whined.

"No she's not. We gotta go!" he barked.

"I don't want to..."

"She's not scary! Let's go!" he roared.

Then he smacked me.

My whole body trembled. There was a long silence. A stream of tears ran down my face as he rebuked me for speaking out and not listening to him. After watching him walk proudly into the shallow, narrow hallway and into his room, I stood silent and frozen for a long period.

My dad would smack me around the head quite often. It happened especially during fourth and fifth grade.

Understanding the severity of the damage, sometimes my mom would walk into my room to try to comfort me which always surprised me, but he hit her too. She would agree with me that his behavior was wrong, yet she told me to not to tell my school teachers and friends about it, or call 911. To my mom, image was everything.

"If you tell your best friend Crystal, she will tell her parents, and they might call authorities. So would the teachers. Then your father will go to jail, and you will never see him again," she cautiously explained.

I believed my mom, not recognizing her deception until my college years. Taking her advice, I never shared what was going on at home with anyone, keeping it a highly-guarded secret. Instead, as a coping mechanism, I cut off my dad. I did what a nine year-old could do. I stopped speaking to him.

After he began hitting me with excessive force, I looked at him as if he was a ferocious beast. I was scared of my own father. Because of the furious look I discerned on his face every morning, my mind ceaselessly attacked me on any occasion. Even sitting next to him for dinner rocked my soul inside and out. Every night when he arrived home from work, I fled to my room at a speed of light. When my mom called me for dinner, I ate as quickly as I could, with my heart beating insanely, so I could rush back to my room as quickly as possible.

Whenever my mom mentioned that she was going to leave the house to go grocery shopping or get gas, I rushed out of the house with her to avoid being alone with him. One time, when my mom did leave me alone with him, and I was literally frozen. We were watching television and I robotically walked over to the fridge to give him anything he demanded, whenever he asked.

Even being with him at a distance was nerve-racking. I never knew if, out of nowhere he would scream or throw something if he did not get what he wanted right away. I had witnessed my dad throwing objects at my mom during aggressive arguments. I remember the very night when I heard an extremely loud noise and my mom's shrieking voice in the kitchen. After a period of silence, I watched my dad slowly walk across the hallway and into the bedroom.

Panting in fear, I cautiously withdrew from the living room, step by step, and moved towards the kitchen, trying not to breathe too heavily in case he heard it. There, I discovered my mom lying on the floor, facedown. My heart was beating rapidly, triggering a surge of panic. I didn't know what to do, whether to tell anyone or remain silent. Although my mom recovered from this incident, that panic stayed within me. I became scared for my own life and not because of cancer. I was only seven-years-old.

BIG BOLD BEAUTIFUL

Chapter 6
Anxiety, Loneliness, and Insecurity

My parents' frequent abuse became a common denominator in silencing myself. My room and my parent's room were next to each other. My heart would beat wildly whenever I heard the footsteps of my parents, especially my mom, walking to the end of the hallway, thinking she would enter my room for something I had done wrong.

My heart rocked like an earthquake when I heard her bark of displeasure.

"Why didn't you place the milk in the fridge exactly as I told you to? Why did you chop the cucumbers so wide?"

Or about my sister, Eunice, who had just turned two.

"Why did you forget to brush your sister's hair? Look at how she looks now!"

My mom would slam the door muttering in Korean,

"Jenn, you can never do one to ten things right."

By the age of ten, all the trust in my parents had gone. They were oppressive and intimidating. It was clear from their words and actions that they did not trust me either, or love me. I didn't think I had any self-esteem.

To avoid being repeatedly mistreated, I began to obey every command my parents gave, and never spoke a word in opposition. I was completely silent when at home with them.

For the most part, I believed that my mom and dad had killed my spirit. I had no one to understand the position I was in. It hurt immensely that I could not share my troubles with Crystal or Laura, or anyone else for that matter. Even if we had talked about such matters, I did not know what my friends would think and did not want them to view my parents in a negative light.

On the side, I didn't know what would happen to me if my parents ever found out that I had shared our family secrets. If only I had known then that my dad needed help, and if I had spoken up perhaps he would have received therapy. But he would have rejected that as effectively as he had rejected me.

Fifth grade was the hardest year of my elementary school life. My fear of failure continued to torture me.

Envy Rolls

Since I had no freedom to do anything at home, I had no courage to explore and try something new. It was just the same miserable routine every day. I grew quite jealous of my younger sister, Eunice, over time because my mom and dad never abused her. Instead, my mom boasted about her to my uncle and grandparents, saying Eunice received endless compliments on her beauty wherever she was out in public.

She said it went to the point where my mom had to tell her friends to stop complimenting Eunice so she would not become too proud and vain. My mom's comments, regarding Eunice's appearance in particular, were a hammering blow to the little girl inside of me whom my mom had once boasted about too, before the cancer had ravaged my head.

Envy took root in me. It caused me to hate my sister and ignore her too.

My only sanctuary was my time with Laura and Crystal. We chatted about popular celebrities we loved; gossiped about kids we disliked, shared our feelings about our school and the teachers. But our conversations never touched on anything that was personal. My reluctance to allow anyone to hear about my wounds built a barrier between me and my friends too.

BIG BOLD BEAUTIFUL

Chapter 7
Search for Approval

When the time for middle school was slowly drawing near, my parents suddenly decided I should have a partial wig to wear at my new school instead of a hat. I was completely taken aback. I could not figure out their reasoning for suggesting it, because I had never shared all about the mocking at school. They did not know about a single hurtful thing said to me outside our home or the pressure of being teased. All they were aware of was that I was very shy and silent—like a mute.

After being hurt regularly without them acknowledging it, my parents never asked how my emotions and mental health were affected by what my peers thought of me. On top of that, my family's inability to buy anything expensive at the time, because of the failed business and my horrific medical costs which they were still paying back, made their decision that much more astonishing, since quality wigs were very expensive.

I eventually learned that their close friends, who knew quite a lot about proper parenting, were the ones who had encouraged my parents to help me with my appearance. Additionally, my parents had been told by neighbors that local kids were picking on me. They would constantly come home hearing of my timidity. When I realized that my parents had taken note of all the advice, I felt a small token of love.

Three months before my graduation from primary

school, a Japanese lady who spoke Korean came over to our house one evening to get started on the wig. First of all, she had to assess my head. I have never forgotten her encouraging words,

"Your daughter has thousand-year hair!"

Her words metaphorically meant that I had strong, shiny, silky hair—and it was the biggest boost to my self-esteem that I had received in a long time.

Good hair ran in my mom's family. My mom was known for her strong, long, and well-nourished hair, which grew quickly and hardly fell out. It was luxurious with a soft texture and I had inherited it.

While preparing to make my handmade wig, the Japanese lady took her time, measuring my bald area, observing my hair color, and looking at the thickness of my hair strands.

She then took a month to carefully sew each strand of hair into the cap and made sure she designed the wig to cover only the area where I was bald. When the wig was completed, she came back and attached the part-weave human hair onto my bald spot with an adhesive. For the first time, I had a full head of hair again. When I looked at myself in the mirror, I did not have a bald spot. I was stunned at how different I looked. I was elated.

This thousand-dollar partial wig was a fortune for my parents, but I wore it every day for thirteen years—from middle school until the end of college. There were many pros and cons of wearing the wig, but in the long run, I was glad to have finally escaped from being labeled as "*Baldy.*"

I may have had a brand new appearance but I was still the same scared me inside. Some of my peers from my primary years were changing schools with me and I was worried they would gossip about me.

I was known to my family, and my school teachers and friends, by a Korean name, Sang Hee. Now I wanted something that was less memorable.

This plan was meant to cover my identity and make me look like an average girl with average hair, instead of a stand-out dysfunctional girl characterized by hair loss, crippled by rejection. Excited, Crystal and I spent the whole day looking for an English name for me. Tired of reviewing the same, generic, common names, I finally decided,

"Let's just stick to Jennifer—Jennifer Kim."

We both agreed to use this simple name.

Over the next few days, I contemplated whether I should share my plan with my parents. I didn't know what they would feel about me leaving behind the name they had chosen for me; I was afraid they would think I was abandoning my Korean roots. I concluded that it would be best if I at least tried, as their support for me would help me a lot.

I slowly and nervously walked over to ask my mom one day, while she was cooking in the kitchen. I tugged on her apron and asked her if she could tell my dad to help me change my name.

She did not say anything for a long time as I held my breath, then she slowly nodded her head. She didn't ask me why, or raise a single objection. To this day, I have no idea what she was thinking, but the best thing was, she had agreed. I felt an enormous relief and was so happy for the rest of the day. When she spoke to my dad the following day, he agreed to my request too. Stunned that both my parents would agree, I looked at them differently. I was not expecting them to be so open-minded. Maybe they had understood some of the hardships I had been through.

On the first day of middle school, my native name was switched to a new American one.

While I could have attended the middle school most students in my community preferred, where there was a large number of Korean students enrolled, I still chose the local zone school.

I really desired to start again, and finally have the chance of a normal school life. However, the anxiety I had developed over the years weighed heavily on my mind. Issues of popularity, cliques, and bullying were loomed large but I simply carried it from one school to another.

Daniel Beard Carter Middle School was daunting. I dragged my feet, my heart pounding with every step, brushing off the sweat from the wig I had on for one of the first time in my life. In the middle of aimlessly walking around the schoolyard and waiting for the school door to open, James Rhee, the boy who had supported me in the church, locked eyes with me and said,

"Hey, you're Sang Hee! You go to this school with me now?"

"No, I'm Jennifer," I nervously replied.

"Yes, you are—you're Sang Hee!" he said cheerfully.

"No, I'm Jennifer!" I stomped away, abashed. My new disguise had fallen at the first hurdle. I walked rapidly in search of my new classroom.

The students in my school came from multiple ethnic and religious backgrounds including Chinese, Filipino, Vietnamese, Taiwanese, Bengali, Islamic, and Hispanic. It is a veritable cultural melting pot.

As soon as the school year began, I observed some of the students forming their own circles, so I chose to fit into one. I was welcomed by some Hispanic girls' and I let myself be absorbed into their group. I wanted to fit in a clique rather than make only one friend or be viewed as an outsider. I was seeking for approval and acceptance, because I had so little of it at home and in primary school.

I was so shy I didn't say much at first but the group of six didn't expect me to. I was most comfortable and casual around Amanda. Our frequencies connected very well. I was also surprised to meet Maria, who was similar in height as me, something we immediately bonded over.

The conversation was all about teachers, boys, and our lives in general. We often loitered in the backyard after school to watch boys play basketball and admire those who could play well.

Amanda and I would gossip all the way home from school, and at weekends we would hang out together at each other's house and in neighborhood parks. But one day Amanda announced that she and her entire family were moving to Indiana.

I panicked. Amanda had become my first real friend after Crystal and Laura and I was much closer to her than any of the others. I felt like yet again the rug was to be pulled out from under my feet. I knew that even if I somehow managed to maintain a long-distance friendship with her, it just would not be the same without having her physically next to me. However, there was just not much I could do about the situation. The other girls were not so nice to me after Amanda left. I felt that I no longer belonged there as I had been too dependent on Amanda.

My fear and loneliness returned when Maria began comparing my height to hers. She labeled me a *"Midget."* I did not understand why when she was only as tall as me.

Of course we would all get bigger as time went on. Crystal who had been three inches shorter than me was suddenly three inches taller; the same height as Laura. Though Crystal witnessed the significant change in height, she remained a humble loyal friend for me, never comparing her height to mine in superiority. Still, I was worried I would be left behind without a growth spurt.

I was aware of my height issues because I never drank milk. I had become lactose intolerant after the radiation treatment I had undergone, which in turn stunted my growth. At the age of seven, any kind of milk including chocolate or strawberry milk upset my digestive system. The thought of eating cheese made me want to gag, and even its smell tortured me. My appetite had also vanished with the cancer treatment.

On top of that, my parents couldn't afford to help me stay physically fit by sending me to a gym to participate in sports. As a result, I had only grown to be 4'7" by the time I reached middle school. In adulthood I am currently 4'9".

Maria's harshness turned to bullying. She pushed me against the wall and cut in line in front of me in the school cafeteria. During the outdoor gym period, she demanded I stay in the corner of the courtyard so she and her friends could have a conversation in Spanish together. After much thought, I walked up to her and asked why she was distancing me from the group.

"Because you are Korean," she replied.

So we were back to that.

She mentioned that since I was a different ethnicity, her friends felt uncomfortable but initially did not mind. As for Maria, she became extremely bothered by the way her clique appeared, compared to the other Hispanic cliques. It hurt to know that she wanted me to stay out of her circle of friends, but I accepted it.

After they excluded me, I never walked near them again. I tried to stay as far away as possible, and pretended I couldn't hear them scoffing and sneering at my appearance. At least I had been there before, and I just put my bubble back up and tried to keep going. It seemed my new name and my new wig were not enough to turn my life around. Then the wig became an issue too.

The adhesive would wear off and the wig would slip, exposing my bald patch. The lady advised me to reattach it every three months but it started to slide off every three weeks or so with no warning. When I looked in the mirror in the bright sunlight, I could detect if it was out of place or not. I was constantly terrified it would suddenly fall off and my awful secret would be exposed. My dad was willing to help but I was so afraid he would start complaining about the cost of the glue.

I tried to hide any uncovered spots with my own hair so that even if it came loose the area would be covered. But there was not enough hair to cover the entire bald area.

One day, while I was waiting in line for lunch, Maria approached me and abruptly asked,

"Jenn, why is this area bald? Did your dad hit you so hard you lost your hair?"

I gasped. *How did she know my dad hit me?*

"I was diagnosed with brain cancer...." I answered quietly, with my whole body trembling.

This was all I could say. I would have wept if I had shared anything more with her. To my surprise, her expression suddenly softened, and she comforted me, putting her hands on my shoulders and softly massaging them. But this was my last chat with her. Curious to know for myself if the wig was out of place, the very next day I used a mirror on one side and another mirror on the other side in the sunlight to view the bald area. Shocked, I made out that the wig had slid down an inch from my hairline. Since then, I was extremely careful to wash my hair, brushing each strand slowly.

My treatment at home was not that much better than at school. I had developed moles on my face and body as a result of the chemotherapy and radiation, and summers spent in the sun. I was shocked at first but didn't take them seriously. My mom and dad had them too. But my mom's incessant name-calling was a push towards shame.

Shortly after I started middle school, my mom began jokingly describing my face. She even compared the shape of my face to my sister's, mentioning my round face and my sister's slim face.

"Come out, mole-faced girl!" She would shout.

It made my five-year-old sister laugh so she started copying her as well.

One day, while I was watching television, Eunice walked up to me and stared at my face.

"What are you doing?" I asked.

"Playing a game," she said.

Glaring at her, I asked, "What game is it?"

"Connecting the dots," she said, laughing.

Furious at her naive words, I pushed her aside and rushed to my room. My mom's rude commentaries led me to believe that people would judge not only my head but also my face. I began to feel very sorry for myself.

In the middle of the year, my parents opened their very own nail salon and gave me a tour of it. My mom showed me around the nail salon stations and the waxing room. After excitedly explaining how she had learned to wax eyebrows, my mom asked if I wanted my eyebrows waxed. After seeing the smile on her face, I agreed, not knowing I was setting myself up for more insults.

"You have eyebrows just like your dad. It's so hard to find a good shape. If only you had eyebrows like mine, it would be so much easier to discern the natural arch and do this for you," she said, frowning.

After the waxing was completed, I stood up to see my new eyebrows in the mirror, expecting to find new beauty in them. As I stared at a pair of mismatched eyebrows, my heart shrank.

The effects of my mom's criticism of my physical appearance had reached her peak. I saw how ugly I was in that mirror so I refused to look at myself in any mirror again. I covered up the one in my room with a sheet.

BIG BOLD BEAUTIFUL

Chapter 8
Sing It Out

Music was my only comfort, reducing the tension in my head and making me feel more resilient. I learned to use music as an escape.

Chorus was my favorite subject. I joyfully rushed to the chorus room as soon as the bell rang for change of lessons, just to be fully prepared. The music teacher, Mrs. Daniels, was big-boned and obese, but she was also humorous, bubbly, and a talented conductor. I was a soprano, and the sopranos were seated on the right side of the class, while the altos were on the left.

The instant Mrs. Daniels' lessons began, I was fully myself— passionate and so loud that my high-pitched voice stood out above the entire class. Whenever I left her class, after the period ended, Mrs. Daniels would often compliment my passionate soul for singing. She even told the other teachers about me.

During one session, she shouted out to a math teacher,

"The voice from this girl kicked it out!"

That boosted my self-esteem no end. But what I gained in Mrs. Daniel's class, I lost at other times.

One day in eighth grade, while I was walking home, a ninth-grade Chinese boy, Tom, walked by me, shocked to notice my height. At 5'1", he was short himself. He fell into step beside and started asking why I was so small. Assuming my growth stunt stemmed from my parents' DNA, he asked about the height of my parents and grandparents. Then he rudely mocked my height by calling me "*Shorty*," "*Dwarf*," and "*Midget*." I didn't say a word since I was so timid to speak out. I didn't wish to talk to him anymore, but that didn't stop him trying to make me the laughing stock of the same block, all day every day after that. He brought his friends to point at me at and laugh.

"Hey, look at this girl! Can you believe how short she is? And she says she's in the eighth grade!"

I always ended up running away in tears, as they watched, laughing at my escape. One day after school, Tom ran over to me and asked,

"Jenn, can I invite you to my house for dinner this Sunday? I want to show my parents how small you are."

Furious, I immediately ran home after he said this. I continued to do so every day after school, running all five blocks as quickly as I could. After being treated like I was nothing, I refused to listen to the group of boys mistreating me this way.

I sensed at this point in my life I needed to just disappear and get as far away as possible from all the negative people that surrounded me. I felt trapped in my miserable life. I longed for my parents to move to the Long Island suburbs, close to Flushing, but my parents were trapped as much as I was. Their nail salon was doing very well, and extremely profitable, but my medical debts were a yoke around their necks. I could not forget what my mom told me as a seven year-old,

"We will be paying off your medical bills every month for the rest of our lives."

So I endured school, and once I reached home, I stayed home. Watching Korean dramas became a comfort zone, but the pain was inescapable. I felt so withdrawn that all I could do was lose myself in the dramas as a defense against my emotional stress.

Music De-Stresser

On the weekends, I did emerge to go to karaoke lounges with Crystal. Crystal loved to sing as much as I did. It was easy for us to attend since an ID card was not required and a lot cheaper during the day. After the employee opened a special room for us, I immediately felt a sense of belonging whenever I grabbed the microphone.

I used music to fill the cavern of stress the way other people used smoking and alcohol, or drugs—every time the risk of cancer popped into my head, I discarded the idea.

* * * * * * * * *

Our city Department of Education standards allowed middle school students to stay behind until their freshman year ended, which I did because of my dad's strong demands. I chose to stay because of my tremendous fear of peers. I figured, *if middle school was tough to endure, how much more pressure would I bear when I enter high school, where there would be a larger population that is creative in its means of hurting others?* Those of us who were staying could not take part in the middle school graduation ceremony. I was glad I did not have to partake in the ceremony.

While practicing our graduation song, my music teacher asked if I would like to sing as a soloist during the performance. For a moment I jumped out of excitement. But then I realized it meant that the entire audience would watch me agonizingly sweat and stutter as I sang, just as I had done on multiple occasions when I had to speak during individual or even group presentations in class. Smiling, I shook my head in response and walked out of class.

Two months before my graduation ceremony, a letter arrived from school. It was a card from the Parent-Teacher Association. To show my thanks and to meet my beneficiaries in public, the card stated that I should attend the night show. Again, I chose not to.

After missing the performance, a counselor pulled me out of class to write a letter of apology and thanks for the gift of five hundred dollars. I was deeply apologetic to the parents and teachers of the school, but I was confused by the meaning of the gift. Was it because I was short or because I had a high grade-point average? I found out from the counselor that the PTA had chosen me as a unique student who stood out. Deeply humbled after hearing this, I wrote my letter of thanksgiving.

Apparently, my singing in the chorus during our school's music performances had been outstanding and the parents who offered the prize thought my talent should be rewarded. I was grateful to hear this, but on the side, I doubted the sincerity of their praise. It made sense I stood out— always first in line walking to the stage at every performance. However, uniqueness was not necessarily a positive thing to me because of my life's experiences.

That night, I showed the check to my dad. The school stated that the gift was to be used for myself, but that did not happen.

The following week, my dad took me to the local bank and presented me to his manager. Within ten minutes my money was deposited into his bank account. I never saw the money again. I was angry but I didn't say anything. I hoped he would use it to pay off their rent or for some logistics.

However, for three weeks my dad came home late practically every night, so I realized it was going on to dinner and drinks with his friends. For the first time this captured my concept of parents, how easily they can take advantage of their own children.

BIG BOLD BEAUTIFUL

Chapter 9
Cliques A Norm

As graduation from middle school drew near towards the end of my freshmen year, panic kicked in. I had heard that high schools were much bigger than middle schools, which meant that there would be a larger student population in comparison to my middle school. I predicted a greater number of peers would use their power to harm and threaten me.

I had also learned that they were far more aggressive in their bullying tactics. Expecting this outcome as inevitable, I fought against my inescapable pain and suffered from insomnia all summer. I was enrolled in Bayside High School as my zoned school in the fall.

I began taking a local bus for the first time; it was the Q28 bus that dropped us directly in front of the entrance of the school building. I was hesitant to take the bus at first, after noticing the stern cold demeanor of bus drivers every school day. They would shout at the students to move to the back of the bus. Their harsh tones terrified me, except for one driver. He displayed a calm expression. Once we arrived at our stop, he would smile at us as we hopped off the bus. He never shouted at us, just encouraged us.

"Move to the back everyone, you see more space in the back, or else other students won't get home in time as you can." he said nicely.

We listened to him and did as we were told. Every time I met him at the scheduled bus time, relief would bubble up inside my chest. Just before walking out of the bus door, passing by his driver's seat, I always longed to say thank you, but never did. I was afraid that students would laugh at my high-pitched voice or the fact I was the only one thanking him. All the more, my heart was disappointed. I gave in to my fears, as I always did.

Beginning of School

The males at Bayside High School looked like utter giants. They were at least a foot taller than me. I remember watching male students with an average height of 5'9" to 5'11" passing by me in the hallway. It helped that there were around 2,200 at the school, of all different ethnic races. I somehow managed to remain largely undetected and was taken by surprise I wasn't called out in my sophomore year.

I began to feel more comfortable than ever before—entering and leaving the classroom in between periods. I negotiated the girls' bathroom, the cafeteria line and the bus to and from school without my usual fears.

I had a strong desire to fit in. I was craving attention, popularity, and approval to encounter a sense of worth even once. Therefore, I looked intensely to connect with Korean students. Remembering the reason that Maria said that I did not fit in with her clique, in her ethnic group, I thought I should try to connect with Koreans. But it was not as easy as I thought. They all seemed pretty silent. I watched them sit quietly in class without saying a word to me or any other classmates.

Sitting in the chorus room after I had passed the vocal audition, I met three Korean girls who were low altos to my soprano. Each time we met in chorus, we greeted each other with a "hey" before taking our seats and remaining silent, looking as nervous as I was. That was all the communication we had though, never having a chance to develop a closer friendship.

After school ended, I followed the students to the bus and hopped on, watching everyone on the sidelines. I was an observer now. I couldn't work out why all the Koreans on the bus were so quiet. We were not a quiet race by nature, as my penchant for singing showed. I assumed they were all as intimidated as I was by their parents and grandparents.

Once, when I was at a lunch table sitting with a couple of students from diverse ethnic groups, I met a Korean boy named Matt. He looked like a man I had seen in a Korean drama—tall, light, and handsome. However, I was more attracted to him because of his friendliness. He became my crush. I kept this secret to myself, telling absolutely no one about how much I liked him, except Crystal, who was attending a different school. The fear of rejection was my personality's touchstone.

I feared that if I told Matt of my interest, I would expect an immediate "no" based on my figure, baldness, and ugliness. These insecurities pressured me into suppressing my feelings. I knew what the others would say if they found out too.

"That girl has a crush on Matt? That girl is too short to be dating Matt. She's not a good fit for him."

Besides, I would never have told him anyway. In all the Korean dramas it was the man who asked the girl out. And I knew I could never be the heroine of his dreams. In the television shows, most women were seductive, flirtatious, and cunning. I didn't see myself like that at all. I refused to have even one student watch me flirt with a guy and notice

I have a crush on him. Gossip was also one of my greatest agony and I didn't want anyone to spread rumors of my interest in Matt.

I did sense from time to time that Matt was aware of my feelings for him. My cheeks flushed whenever he approached, or when he called my name,

"What's up, Shorty Jenn?"

The term *"Shorty"* was trendy around that time, especially for small girls. It sounded like a term of endearment to me.

Whenever Matt joined our table, I would fall silent. I would reply back with a "hi" and say no more. I was shy to talk to him in person, but bold enough to communicate through online chats and in chatrooms. He stayed my crush throughout the entire school year. I actually began to look forward to going to school.

The school population grew exponentially in my junior year because a school nearby closed down. A majority of the new students were African-American. I sensed that most of the Asians were intimidated by them. Their loud antagonism toward Asians had been widespread since my younger years.

I could remember being a four-year-old, sitting in the backseat of our car at a red light in the Bronx, and we were stopped next to a beat-up car, seemingly filled with young black men. They were blasting out rap music on the car radio, nodding their heads up and down to the beat while staring at us with ferocious expressions. When the lights changed they drove away, shouting gibberish, pretend-Chinese words at us. My mom had sat frozen while I had been more interested by their hairdos. When they were gone my mom relaxed, pouring out all her terror and dismay to my dad.

My experiences in the Bronx stayed with me. I was always acutely aware of the threat of people gathering in groups. But with the new influx to the school came new cliques. The cliques were usually exclusively male or female, a mix of both girls and boys, or more commonly, multiple boys with only one girl.

The Korean students began to interact with a group of individuals that were only of their ethnic group. Among those who had just emigrated from Korea also formed their own cliques. They were generally secluded from bonding with the average Korean-Americans since they were different from those of us born and raised in America. American-born Koreans labeled these newcomers FOBs, or Fresh Off the Boat, judging them for their lack of their linguistic skill and cultural status.

I can still remember a group of FOBs who stood in a circle in a separate area of the cafeteria or the schoolyard, deliberately isolating themselves from the Korean-American cliques.

Some of the students didn't belong to a group so we were just as isolated—including me. Walking past each social circle sitting at their designated lunch table or waiting for the school door to open each day, I wondered how much harder it would be to deal with cliques in college or at work as an employee when finding a "friend" is hard enough. I believed I did not fit in with Korean-Americans, even though I was considered one of them. Still desperate to fit into any social circle, I decided to identify myself as an FOB.

As an FOB, I could follow their cultural background. I was good at Korean, thanks to my obsession with Korean dramas. The fact that I grew up in Flushing— a Korean oriented city, also helped. So, that is how a girl who had tried so hard not to be identified as Korean, even to the point of changing her name, began trying to make friends with the most obviously Korean students at the school. Since I fit the criteria, I had joined cliques with the girls—Emma, Iris, and Natalie. I had become friends with them after meeting Emma in the gym. She was friendly, approachable, and outgoing, so when she asked me to sit with her and her friends at lunch, I agreed.

After joining them regularly at the lunch table, I began to feel that I had found a place where I belonged. I wanted to gain confidence from someone, to hear anyone's words of affirmation instead of the long-term, derogatory comments from peers. But this never happened. Instead, there was this nagging feeling that I was an intruder.

Natalie and I were usually the first to arrive. I always spoke first, which was totally new for me, but if I didn't Natalie wouldn't say anything. When Emma was first to arrive after her, I would watch Natalie speak excitingly to her. Emma would speak but generally with others and rarely made eye contact with me, which was odd given she had invited me in the first place. My silence started to become pronounced after that.

I listened to their conversations about their weekends with their friends, their latest crush on a guy, or rivalry between the Korean-Americans and the FOBs. But I was definitely on the outside.

One day, the girls asked me to pronounce a word.

"Coney Island," I said with a silent 's'.

Then they started cracking up, in laughter at Natalie.

"I get it!" she said, laughing with them.

With summer approaching, all they talked about was Coney Island and the beach. Listening to their chats every lunch period, I assumed all of us would plan on visiting the beach sometime soon. Then one Monday at school, it was obvious they had all already been, without me.

"Was the sand nice?" asked Emma.

"The waves were beautiful," replied Natalie.

"I wished I could've worn a bikini though. My swimsuit wasn't too tight."

I asked myself why they had not invited me. Then my generalization was that I was small, so I did not fit in. I could, of course, have asked them to hang out with me randomly during the weekends, but that thought never crossed my mind. I was too shy to ask. I was afraid I would hear,

"Sorry, Jenn, I made plans with my friend, so maybe next time."

I started to withdraw and use the group as a come-and-go tactic at the lunch table, not to feel, or look so isolated, nor be forced to eat alone. As the loneliness inside of me deepened, I chose to avoid them as the new semester began. I did not want to join a clique that excludes others often and constantly leans on the "leader" of the group.

After my experience with Emma and her friends, the belief kept storing in my head that I would never meet the expectations of others, coming from my appearance that negatively influenced my personality.

The female students never seemed to mock me like the males did, but I sensed that they showed their exclusion by avoiding me. I watched many girls randomly meeting each other between classes, then spending a long time chatting, even if the chat made them late for their next class. When I randomly met someone we generally just said "hi" and then moved on.

I had so wished to find at least one girl who was willing to accept me as a friend; enough to risk the time to talk in the hallway with me, even if it meant being late to class.

Eventually, the thought I kept in my head made it clear, *I can never find a friend who I can trust. I can find no friend with a heart to stick with me and care to know me more despite my appearance.* Because I didn't know how to start a conversation well, the social neglect of the females made me feel envious and inadequate.

As for the males, that was a different story.

Chapter 10
Fashion Is Key

As majority of the students were average height, I wasn't. I remained one of the shortest people in school. The belittling of my height became more immense in the middle of my junior year.

Korean boys would look down at me as we passed in the hallway and say, "Woah!" while the African-American boys would shout, "Dang," and then laugh and smirk as they walked away. Occasionally, someone walking in the opposite direction would tap my head while passing by. When this happened, I walked on in silence, but deep inside I fought to ignore the pain, rubbing my eyes, to keep even one tear from rolling down my cheeks.

Keeping up with fashion trends was not easy when one was so small either, or wore a wig. North Face jackets and dead straight hair had become the must haves in my late high school years, especially for Korean females. It was called *"magic straight hair"*— long, silky, and super-straight. Wherever I walked, whether to school or in my neighborhood, I noticed that pretty much all adolescents walked out their door wearing a North Face jacket and nearly all Korean girls passing by with their *"magic straight hair."*

I searched for a North Face jacket and desired the same hair as the others. I thought it might help me be socially accepted and maintain group identity. Unfortunately, the jackets were not available in my size and as for straight hair, there was no way for each strand of hair in my wig to stay in place and look straight. Besides, my natural hair was growing faster than usual, so the imbalance in length between the wig and the human hair would have been easily identifiable if it was ramrod straight.

So I continued to go to school in an ordinary jacket, with my shoulder-length hair pinned half up in the front, to hide my wig. Now, I stood out even more.

I was ashamed to be deemed to have poor fashion sense and a bad hairdo. It did not look like a big deal if a Korean girl saw a Muslim girl wearing a headscarf or a Hispanic girl with curly hair since this was accepted as a religious or cultural choice.

But the fact that I did not look like a typical Korean girl, with long, straight hair, I felt it would be difficult for the Korean students to accept me. I knew this since Crystal had often discussed it with me and sharing what she heard from her friends. She knew how it would feel knowing she had the hairstyle while I did not.

It brought back the memory of the fifth-grade trend of flared jeans followed by the middle school popularity of baggy jeans. If I had to follow fashion trends, I could never show my personal identity and feel good about myself. It had never when I failed to match flared jeans with the color and style of my hat or baggy jeans with my wig's hairstyle. I believed that my poor fashion, along with my wig and height, had closed doors to others who would never interact with me because of how I looked on the outside.

I knew it was shallow, but fashion was a way of gaining affirmation, and I couldn't follow it. I pictured myself in the future as a powerful, influential woman who puts on makeup, wears skirts, and walks in high heels all the time in order to look good. I deeply felt that my body image would strongly impact my acceptance in a job interview, in the workplace, or even in everyday life. Stressed by this possibility, I chose not to think about it. All I could do was continue to stay surrounded by a multitude of peers and isolate myself and maintain my more reserved stance. It hurt that I could not have a chance to gain "coolness," or even a sense of belonging, yet feel like a loner in school. To comfort myself I turned back to my usual vice: singing.

Crystal and I still went to karaoke often, whenever we had the time and the money. Singing karaoke became a habit I lovingly nourished until the middle of my college years. I was desperate to express my pain by using my voice. It felt good to have a way of conveying my personality. I would sing all the sad R&B songs and let out my loneliness and sadness out through the familiar words and rhythms, in front of an imaginary, appreciative, audience. My karaoke experiences made me feel very relaxed, as if I were a celebrity who was evaluated only by my singing talent, not my looks.

BIG BOLD BEAUTIFUL

Chapter 11
Why Can't I Be Accepted?

My senior year was by far the hardest year of my life. It was truly oppressive. The school population had now doubled to almost 4,000. As far as I can remember, the ethnic makeup of the population was a little over half Asian, with Koreans making up most of that half.

I was surprised at the surge in the number of African-American students, but even more by the new acceptance of each other by the Koreans and the African-Americans.

I watched students from both groups fist bump each other in the corridors, exchanging shout outs.

"What up, nigga?"

"What up, kigga?"

Neither side seemed offended. I wondered how this relation was initiated. I later learned from Crystal and some people that playing basketball and break-dancing together had cemented a new respect between the cultures, at least inside the school walls. But the friendly exchanges took place only among the males.

The overcrowded school made it almost impossible to pass freely in the hallway to get to each class. It felt like being in heavy traffic, moving at less than five miles per hour. In an attempt to move faster, we often shifted our bodies sideways to pass through the crowd more quickly. Our teachers were aware of the problem and they did not say anything if we came late to class.

There were so many I don't think most of the student body remembered all the names of the people in our year. But it seemed everyone knew me distinctly enough, labeling me as the,

"*Super-Short Asian Girl*" or "*The Girl with the Bun*," reminding me of the days when John in nursery school was labeled as,

"*The Boy with the Lion King Cap.*"

This association of my identity with the characteristics that devastated me was the beginning of my oppression—a new oppression. Near the beginning of the year, I started putting my hair into a bun after obsessing over the "magic straight hair", which later affected my mind of how my wig looked. I feared judgment from my peers since they could easily see my bald spot as they passed me in the overcrowded hallways. Not once did I want to be called a "*Baldy*" again. I couldn't stop hearing,

"Dang, small midget," or "Woah,"

accompanied by their harsh laughter every class period. I hated walking silently through the hallways with the people feeling they had the right to tap me on the head. The longer I remained silent, the greater I wanted to yell at them to stop with their rude remarks and the insensitive tapping. But fear stole my voice, keeping me from standing up for myself.

It seemed I remained invisible to the girls, but visible enough for the Korean boys to ridicule me on a daily basis. The female FOB acquaintances started talking with the new friends they had found in every class, all the while excluding me. This was despite all my efforts to reverse this trend. My turmoil increased with the added fears of possible verbal or physical attacks, or of rumors spreading throughout the entire school. Over the course of the school year, I remained reserved during every class period, sitting in the back, just as some boys did.

Unreliable Friend's Friends

I looked at everyone as an enemy rather than as a fellow student. Whenever I returned home from school, I would weep miserably for an hour or more before turning to my Korean dramas. I realized that I would rather hide under a shell than face emotional torment. I slowly became attached to these dramas that mirrored the effects of real life, including relationships with friends and family.

As most storylines portrayed characters that I could relate to, I associated myself with their loneliness, rejection, indifference, or betrayal. Using these dramas as an escape from reality, I couldn't help but be naturally drawn to each episode. But finally, in the middle of the year, I actually made a friend, thanks to Crystal. As my new friend Jane and I slowly drew close to each other. Jane was one of the nicest people I had ever met, and she had an absolute lack of any sense of judgment. We became so tight that it made me cut classes to meet her in her neighborhood.

She introduced me to her boyfriend, Daniel. We began to hang out after school. It was lovely and friendly. But then, like with everything in my life, something happened to ruin it. Nothing ever lasted.

One day, Daniel walked in with a friend. John was tall and pleasant looking. But I knew from first words he was never a nice guy. I will never forget his first impression of me. He took one look at me and cracked up.

"You're seventeen? No way! You don't even look like a teenager."

"C'mon, Daniel. You're lying. Listen to her high-pitched voice!"

"Wow, Jane—that's so nice of you to make a midget your friend."

His remarks pierced my heart, but I chose to ignore his taunting. I tried to avoid him as much as possible but Daniel kept including him in our group, no matter how much Jane told him not to. My heart would trigger the minute I heard that Daniel was coming over to Jane's house with John. Each time we met, I never left his presence without hearing mocking laughter and harsh remarks like, "Hey, midget."

One day, I was sitting on a couch with John standing in front of me. His eyes gleamed after looking at me for a long time. Suddenly, he announced to Jane and Daniel,

"Hey guys, let's make a video of Jenn dressed up as a baby. We could put a bib around her neck and feed her milk with a bottle. I'll be the father, and as soon as I remove her milk bottle, let's record her crying!"

Upon hearing this, I felt abandoned by my friends, thinking, *Why didn't they look out for me?* I couldn't describe the hurt I felt because Jane and Dan never responded or even ask if I was okay. I burst into tears as soon as I arrived home, feeling like a loser. I was reluctant to confront Jane for fear of losing her friendship. John's ludicrous words made me go straight back to feeling worthless and at the end fall into depression.

What's My Identity?

On top of everything that was already going on, I was also subject to the trauma of assault and attempted rape. The quiet neighborhood I lived in, close to my middle school, was known to be unsafe for young Asian girls. Many Hispanic men loitered on the streets. Whenever a girl passed by on the other side of the block, they would often try to hit on her by shouting out in Spanish. All of us were advised to protect ourselves from becoming the target of their sexual harassment or even sexual assault by others who, unfortunately, spoke from experience. I thought I had taken sufficient precautions and ignored their warnings about the area.

But I was totally wrong.

One day as I was walking alone to a location a few blocks from my house, I was approached suddenly by a tall, thin Hispanic man who started talking to me in Spanish. I told him I did not understand what he was saying, but he continued to talk to me. Then I thought I heard him say something in English.

"Five hundred?" I asked, confused.

At that point, using his left index finger and thumb, he made a circle. Then, he inserted his right index finger into the circle. When he did this, I finally discerned what he was talking about—sex.

I had finally connected the dots and understood that he wanted to have sex with me for money. After realizing this, I shivered and yelled out, "No!" and ran away from him, afraid that he might capture me.

I was still a virgin and the man's approach repulsed me, not that I would have been interested if I wasn't, but his graphic illustration of what sex looked like and the leer on his face made me feel dirty on its own.

Soon after this horrifying event, I was walking alone, once again, in the same area, when a short, big-boned Hispanic man appeared out of nowhere and forcefully grabbed my shoulder from behind. He pushed me against a fence under cover of a tree and vigorously forced himself against me. I could feel his genitals through his clothing. I tried to wrestle him off of me, but he was simply too strong to push away. So horrified that this was going on, I suddenly remembered a conversation in the school cafeteria where a girl had said that if a man ever got fresh, the best thing to do was kick him in the groin.

I swung my legs to kick him. I tried my best, careful not to hurt my leg. I only managed to kick him ferociously in the thighs with both of my legs. In obvious pain, he loosened his hold on me. I seized this opportunity to release myself from his grip and escaped.

Chapter 12
It's Too Much

These two incidents left me traumatized. I carried my secret alone. I was totally confused by my identity. *Am I hated for my looks or overly loved for my looks? Why can't I just be accepted?*

I wanted to tell my few friends and my mom about my wounds to reveal that I was dying inside, but I was too ashamed to do so. I did not want to attract any more judgmental remarks from the people in my life.

My mom was having enough problems with my dad who could never stay sober in or out of home. It was hard to forget my dad walking home late when I was young, strongly unsteady and tipsy, but it worsened. He had started a real estate business which had not run successfully and lost more than he had from the beginning. He had met a friend who he played golf with who also loved to drink. They would often meet together highly intoxicated to relieve their stress.

My dad was usually a quiet man but whenever he came home drunk he grew garrulous, loudly ranting about the debt from my medical expenses, which were still crippling their finances. This was how I incidentally learned about my dad's feelings at the time. It did not help my own guilt and only deepened my depression.

Another event added scars greater than those that John had caused. I could never forget the hurt and the damage inflicted on me that day.

I started studying for my SAT exams at an academy on the weekends. One day I went to study there on a school day, so I had to take a different bus than I usually took. This bus traveled in the direction of Jamaica, a neighborhood made up primarily of African-American residents. There weren't many riders once I hopped on, but it began to fill up as the bus driver waited. He asked the students to move toward the back to let everyone on. I ended up in the back rows with mainly African-American male students. There were hardly any female students on the bus. As my stop drew near, I couldn't stop my heart banging nervously. I was scared to have the students look at me and draw attention to my height.

I was too short to reach the yellow button on the back door to request my stop, and I wasn't strong enough to open the back door anyway, so I decided that I should face the mocking in order to make my way to the front of the bus to get off. It was worse than I had predicted.

"Excuse me," I said softly in an attempt to push my way through.

"Woahhhhhhh," chanted the crowd.

"Look at this Asian Midget!" I heard someone shout.

I was not in the position to protest, so I endured the torment, painfully taking each step as I winced at every damaging statement hurled at me. I felt like each boy was stabbing my heart with a pocket knife. Itching for the front door, I took bigger steps in an attempt to get off faster.

As soon as I escaped the bus, and my heart rate was easing back to normal, I turned to watch the bus drive away, and the last thing I heard was from a kid in the back of the bus, who stuck his head out the window and shouted,

"Bye, Chino!"

Unable to handle the disgrace, I burst into tears in the middle of the street, walking slowly through the quiet neighborhood with my head down to hide my tears.

I Am Totally Inadequate

Never had I felt so mistreated in my entire life—more like a rejected dog than an average human. I hated my body from head to toe. The sense of rejection permeated my heart. I never dared to try anything new. I was firmly of the belief that I was inadequate to give anything a shot, no matter my inclinations.

I was absolutely convinced I could never learn to play the guitar or piano well due to my small hands and short fingers. I had no reason to learn to ride a bike or drive a car because my short legs could not reach the pedals. I could never look good as a dancer because of my super skinny frame—after all, I would look like a dancing child. I thought I could never even be a good cook—the food would never taste good. There was no point speaking or performing in public as no one would look past my height. I reminded myself of my mom's angry words as I clung to my pessimism,

"Jenn can't do anything right."

Self-doubt became a constant in my life. As a result of the extreme judgment and the hostility of my peers— especially males—I was deeply persuaded I would never be loved by a man. The desire for marriage was never in my mind. My perceived lack of beauty would never qualify me for a man's attention.

My social awkwardness grew worse over time, but it did not matter to me. In school, I never ate lunch in order to avoid waiting in line and having people behind me stare at my bald spot or comment on my height. Whenever I was crossing the street, I believed as if the drivers of the waiting cars were staring at my height or judging my tiny feet as I walked by. As a sized-two female passing by with an adult-sized shoes or heels, they would chuckle or giggle at the imbalance of my appearance. I highly detested that even if it were intended for good means.

Ten minutes before my class periods ended I would prepare everything to run out of the classroom as soon as the bell rang, to get to the next class as quickly as possible, to avoid even one remark in the hallway. I did not mind to be the first one always in the room. As soon as school ended, I rushed out of the building to reach the bus station first, instead of hanging out in the schoolyard as most students did. As soon as I hopped on the bus, I sat on the first seat in the front, and didn't meet anybody's eye, creating a distinct boundary between myself and anyone from school who might approach me. I also created the same boundary at home, between myself and my parents, rushing to my room just before they arrived home from work. I would only come out for dinner, otherwise, I stayed in my room. It felt safer there.

Chapter 13
Drama as My Safe Zone

Loneliness was my constant companion. I continued to indulge in Korean dramas as a place to hide my pain. I would binge watch them on the weekends, for twelve hours straight. I was enslaved to each episode, using them to make myself feel safer. They became my voice.

I said that I didn't need anyone, and would never have a romance, but in truth I craved love just like the girls in the dramas. I had gone from craving parental love to craving the love of someone who would be there just for me.

I fantasized about a handsome man, like Matt, who would love me in spite of my appearance; take care of me, speak loving words, and plan dates for me. I dreamed of never feeling alone and rejected by a man.

Despite the addiction, I hated myself more with every day that passed by. I felt exceedingly hideous compared to the beautiful women who the handsome men were attracted to in the Korean dramas.

It worsened when my mom would rant about my complete silence at home, comparing me to my nine-year-old sister.

"Why are you so quiet when your sister is not? She's always smiling and you are not. Why can't you be more like Eunice?"

I couldn't believe she couldn't see it. I wanted to scream at the top of my lungs that all the things that had happened to me had not happened to Eunice. The cancer; the stunted growth; the bullying; the detachment of my parents.

How was I supposed to cope with the stress and the deep scars of my past?

I wanted to do anything that could possibly detach my soul from my body. I hated myself so much that the thought of ending my life ran through my head like crazy. I had church friends and acquaintances, and only two close friends whom I believed I could be completely honest with.

I was too proud to share the truth with anyone, just as my mom was too proud to share the truth of her own problems with her family and friends, claiming it would irritate them. In the same way I felt I had no real friends, my mom had no friends to share her burdens with, either. Therefore, I imitated her philosophy in life but using her way of coping deepened my fears even more.

In addition to my own problems, my mom used me to vent her own upset and frustrations about my dad. She was really too preoccupied with him to focus on me.

My mom's final venting became the last straw. I envisioned myself grabbing a knife and running it down my wrists, slicing the arteries. It would be as real to me as her complaining. I would see the blood gushing out, knowing the amount of time I had to endure was now limited. I would feel the relief. I had considered it for weeks, out of turmoil, three months before my graduation.

Then a thought popped up in my head. *If a needle in my arm had always brought the fear of pain, how much more should I fear a knife? That means living in hell would be more painful than living on this planet...*

Aware I could never escape the agony by forever closing the door on the distress in my life, I faced the tormenting thoughts that were making me go crazy and feel wild inside.

Soberly disheartened, the only thing I could do was cry aloud. And this pattern continued on for days.

I began to think, *If I can't kill myself, then I must continually persevere. But there's no way to end my suffering. No way to get help, no way out. When can this end? What can I do to be granted even the slightest peace? How can I ever stay away from men who inflict such deep wounds upon me?*

Then, suddenly something clicked in me, as if someone was speaking directly to me,

"Wait. You will find freedom if you can endure. Stay faithful, Jenn…. Stay faithful."

I have no idea where it came from. It was like a force from within.

Keeping this thought in the forefront of my mind and heart, I endured this torment until my high school graduation.

BIG BOLD BEAUTIFUL

Chapter 14
Campus Light

I was looking at universities far from home. I wanted to escape my controlling parents and the mockery of those around me. I had a strong desire for the countryside. I wanted to fully recapture the peace I had lost for so long. I thought I could just go away to live in the middle of nowhere, so I wouldn't get hurt by people young and old included.

I was particularly interested in interior design. I had never taken art classes but I had watched my mom design baskets and jewelry when I was five. Whenever I asked her if I could try too, she had responded that I could do this when I was an adult. Well now I almost was, and I wanted to exercise my independence by pursuing the arts in some form.

My dad tried to interfere in my college decision. He wanted me to stay closer to home. He didn't think I was capable of handling a student loan or indeed any debt. But that was the extent of his interest. He never asked about my SAT scores, my GPA, or my consultations with school college counselors.

Despite all my anxiety and fears, something inside of me was telling me it was time to fly free.

There were other factors I had to consider when choosing a university. My average GPA and family's economic status limited my choices. I still had a few New York state schools in mind— far enough for me to gain my own sense of independence while being within an affordable tuition range.

With the help of my school counselor, I found out I was only eligible to attend Queens College since I met the criteria required to qualify for admission to the SEEK Program, designed for students who come from low-income families and are academically unprepared. The SEEK program generously offered great academic and financial support for students who could not afford college without it. Queens College was close to home, which pleased my dad, and the financial aid and grants would cover my tuition and other expenses. Since I did not meet the requirements needed to attend the other universities of my choice, I decided to take up the offer.

Curls Then and Now

For a long time, my mom highly disapproved of my hair tied up in a bun. One month before my high school graduation, my mom and I visited her favorite hair salon and she explained my situation to the hair stylist. My mom told the salonist that she would like for me to have curls again. I followed up with her. I fell asleep while it was done. After two long hours, I woke to long natural curls; not too curly, but rather slightly wavy. Looking straight at the mirror, I was pleasantly surprised by the way I looked. I loved them.

For the first time, I was eager to attend school. Walking to class the next day, many of my classmates complimented me on my new hairstyle, one of the few times I had ever received any compliments. After that, I made sure to get my hair done every six months at the same salon, saving money for it during my college years even if it meant attending without food.

As my high school graduation ceremony was approaching, fear and anxiety filled me again. I worried that I would be judged by the audience in the auditorium because of my oversized gown and large cap. I was alarmed I would hear a random student give a bad shout out. The thought of even walking up the stage to receive my diploma gave me anxiety. I was so self-conscious of how I would appear on graduation day that I couldn't sleep for days. The night before the event, I tossed and turned in my bed praying for a successful walk across the stage.

On the day of the ceremony, I prepared myself, hoping for an enjoyable day with my family. After listening to all the musical performances and student speeches, it was time for all students to receive their diploma. It took a while before our row was about to be escorted to wait in line and go on stage, so I was less panicky. When our row was escorted to wait in line, my heart throbbed. It pulsed even more when the line was drawing closer to the foot of the stage, for our names to be called. I felt my face turn red when my name was about to be called.

"Jennifer Kim."

My name was finally called.

While walking towards the podium, I began to shake uncontrollably. All I heard were clapping hands. I was so delighted I did not hear a single comment from any student shouting out, "Way to go, midget!" or any insults I was subjected to during my high school years. After I shook the Chancellor's hand with my right hand and received my diploma with my left hand, a feeling of sensationalism came over me. I was delighted I didn't encounter a sense of judgment. I felt I could finally put this day behind me. But this feeling quickly vanished after graduation.

During the summer months before college began, I was still so wrought with doubt and fear. The thoughts I had been dwelling on were only on the expansion of the abusive behaviors from others I had experienced during my earlier school years. My mind could not let go of these thoughts and I could not sleep all night. Every night I woke up with cold sweats, panting as if my life was over. I even had nightmares which were always related to my negative experiences in high school.

The insomnia was so severe that the fatigue revealed on my face. In the middle of the summer, my mom slowly asked if I was okay. I nodded and rushed to my room to avoid her from observing me deeply. Then, she asked more frequently when my dark circles were more noticeable. She was aware it didn't come from summer activities that wore me out or staying up watching dramas all night. She knew I never performed these activities.

College was starting soon. One night before bed, my mom walked into my room. She sat down on the bed with me. Then, she earnestly asked for my honesty, the cause of my insomnia. Recognizing her sober-hearted spirit, I let go and confessed.

"I'm scared to attend college. After being treated so badly in high school, I'm scared it may be worse in college. I'm more stressed I might make absolutely no friends there," I stuttered.

Holding my hands, she reassured me with encouraging words. She shared what she had heard from the lifestyle of some of her customers at her nail salon who attend college, and other alumni, as great memories. At the end, she exhorted me to avoid any student who acts immaturely or unwisely.

"Jenn, they are adults now so they should know how to react when they approach someone, not just the disabled but anyone different. So if anyone mocks you, ignore them. You are a woman now. Don't grow close with anyone immature."

Hearing my mom's encouragements, I was relieved. My heart was even more assured after holding a conversation with a church member who was also a college student. I took the courage to confess my feelings, as requested by my mom. Her words also mirrored my mom's, and therefore gave me the desire to attend college. Looking over my class schedule again no longer made me flinch. I was able to sleep through the night after that.

It was the first day of college in the fall, I walked to the campus slowly, with eager intensions. This was the first day of the rest of my life and I felt excited, but apprehensive. The SEEK students were assigned to meet together on the first class. My heart beat faster as I couldn't find the building as well as the right room.

When I did eventually find it, I walked in and found myself face-to-face with two students exactly the same height as me. Bethsaida and Jenny were both short and friendly. The three of us immediately clicked. Not one looked down at the other and attached a label. Finally, after all these years, I had found my soulmates.

Students in each class were welcoming. They asked many questions to get to know me. Not once during the semester did they ask about my height. I was so encouraged they would choose to chat and never hear any contempt at every class session.

Jenny and Jennifer, 2007

Surprisingly, I was opening up my mouth to speak. I did not know how. Many of the SEEK students were not particularly outgoing, rather quiet and reserved. Since I no longer wished to be viewed as a quiet student, even by professors, I took the risk to hold a conversation. I did learn later in educational psychology classes that students coming from low-income backgrounds can be mainly quiet and shy, just as I was. But something in my heart told me not to conform to their behavior and instead search for the opportunity to be myself. I slowly opened up to my classmates, participated during lectures, and chatted with SEEK students during our meals throughout the entire freshman year.

Chapter 15
Slowly Healing

"You're so tiny!"

"You're so petite!"

"You're so small!"

These words constantly echoed at me everywhere I went on campus, especially from the female students. At first, I felt awkward hearing these words because I was never used to people taking it as if it were a good thing. I found it strange that people were smiling at me as they said these things.

No one at college used the term 'short' to describe me. Their contrasting words and body language utterly confused me, making me wonder what their genuine message was. I began to accept their words as implying acceptance of my size rather than undermining me. I was still somewhat distrustful. But my accountable buddies Crystal and Laura helped me carry the positivity.

Boat Ride with Laura At Central Park

I started to venture into the work world. I was employed at a bakery, my first part-time job at the beginning of my freshman year. The employees liked me a lot. They treated me as if I were part of their family. Even the customers were very pleasant. Hence, my fast heartbeat began to slow.

Months later, I received another job in a doctor's office my cousin had recommended me. I was so shocked they had accepted me. It was enjoyable working hard for the patients.

The doctor was surprised I was strong enough to work so well based on my size. He was encouraging and caring. He anticipated I work at his office for at least two years. This was the beginning of my next social endeavor, one that helped boost my confidence level.

In this job, I became a more confident and carefree young woman; more outgoing in my social interactions. After connecting with my identity, I began to explore possible careers.

Interior design was unfortunately out of my reach as Queens College did not have a program for it. I contemplated education since many of my female classmates were enrolled in the field. I enjoyed working with children as we had a lot in common, and I had a special affinity for them. I had gained work experience as a tutor of two children in the summer before college and I realized that children respected me despite my height.

My studies in educational psychology were fascinating, and I realized I would have the empathy required to be a great school teacher.

During the second semester of my freshman year, my English professor discussed drama and theater all semester. She had assigned various activities where we were placed into groups to act out plays. I recall very vividly at the end of a class where my English professor asked me what my field in study would be. I responded that I would like to pursue Elementary Education. She highly recommended I take theater as my second major. It seemed a good fit, given my Korean drama obsession.

As a child who had experienced many emotional situations, in addition to having a fear of social situations, I believed that although I had the potential to pursue theater, it may not be the best or most suitable field for me. I decided I would rather use acting as a creative leisure activity rather than as a career.

Around the same time at the beginning of my freshman year, I was invited to CRU, a Christian campus ministry club. Members were passing out flyers as I passed through my campus one day. Reading the flyer, I instantaneously declined. Even though I was a believer, I had a predetermined judgment already wired in my head, telling me that those who attended the club would ignore me even if they did not explicitly mock me like the girls in high school. Though their perspective on me might change, just as the perspectives of children taller than me had changed, lack of social skills meant that I would not be ready to build a solid friendship with anyone yet. Ultimately, I always chuckled with a "no" every time a student from CRU invited me. I did not decide to attend CRU until much later.

For two years, I was able to enjoy my life. I took a lot of pleasure in using my salary to shop for clothes and shoes, singing at a karaoke bar with Crystal, and paying to watch Korean dramas online. For the first time, I relished buying everything I wanted, just like an average woman. Shopping for clothes and shoes the first time had never been so gratifying. I was also shocked to know I could actually fit into adult clothes available in my size: extra small, extra small petite, or even extra, extra small.

I even had enough salary to go on vacations to Paris with my cousin, who accompanied me as an international student. I confidently crossed the street and showed off my outfit with my nice heels, though still big. I was more comfortable approaching friends on campus. But over time, I felt empty inside, like something was missing. To satisfy this void, I ignored my doubts and made my first visit to CRU in the fall once junior year began.

The only word I could manage while slowly, yet nervously walking in was "hi." The members were welcoming and willing to talk to me, but all I did was smile whenever they attempted to include me in their conversation. I was surprised over how often they used my name, asking questions to get to know me. As soon as the service ended, I was grateful they asked me to dinner.

Even while attending this club, I still had my doubts. If I did not receive the attention I wanted, I assumed they wanted to talk to others. These insecurities prevented me from participating because it fed my fear of failure. I was still the same shy and quiet girl from before, just as they had noticed over time. I never wore a t-shirt because I feared that people would over-analyze my skinny stature. These apprehensive thoughts left me feeling isolated at the club. I presumed that they were not as welcoming as they seemed based on their tone of voice, body language, and seemingly flat attitude.

A fellow club member Michelle, who trained me to share the gospel observed my timidity and pointed out the things that I should work on. She suggested practical issues, comforted me when I became stressed, but also brought up many insecurities Michelle had noticed about me during the year. For a long time, I found it difficult to accept her criticism that reminded me of the frequent criticisms coming from my mom.

When the semester ended, I attended a CRU winter conference, where students from different campuses gather together to connect with God and others. In the middle of a session, Michelle took me out of the auditorium to have a meaningful discussion with me, gently exhorting me about my weaknesses in engaging with people. I was told to stop trying to prove myself in public or feel unrecognized whenever leaders did not greet me. All I could do was cry and listen to her words of discipline.

After she encouraged me to be bold and step away from fear, I took her words to hear. I admitted my wrongs for the first time and looked after the ability to change. I bravely took the initiative to do what I had always desired, which was to pursue missions and share the gospel outside of the United States. By stepping forward with this, I became bold, developing the courage to speak. This affected my desire to stand up as a whole. It helped me grow confident in my everyday interactions over time. Even more, my wounded heart was slowly healing.

BIG BOLD BEAUTIFUL

Chapter 16
To the Right Path

My trip to Thailand was absolutely phenomenal. This was a six-week trip where we traveled as a team of ten, including our leader, Jinnie. The main purpose of this trip was to build cross-cultural friendships. We did this by partnering with members of the same gender and reaching out to students on campus. At the end of each day, the entire team came together to cook and eat. Then, we spent some time in family worship after dinner, sharing what we encountered throughout the day.

TKT Missions Trip, 2010

This was a very memorable team. The "sisters'" eyes could not stop gleaming at me throughout the missions' duration, whether I was sitting or standing. The entire team always complimented my work and social interaction with

the students, which was based on the eyewitness account
provided by my partner, Sunny. She viewed me as a great
encourager and listener and was very supportive of me. I
was so grateful to have a partner like to Sunny to evangelize
with.

Post TKT, Sunny on the right

Peter, a friend from elementary school, was also part of
the team. He made us laugh throughout the whole summer.
His jokes on me and my silly responses strengthened the
team bond.

To know each other more deeply, we shared our
individual life stories. We spent an hour being vulnerable
and sharing our childhood, how we were blessed, enjoying
the fun, memorable moments along with some hardships
we had encountered in the past. We also discussed what our
lives were before we came to believe and how they have
changed since. We reflected on the freedom we have living
in Christ.

I was the last one to share my life's story after drawing
the name out of a hat. This allowed me more time to write
out mine while listening to each of their stories. I was

immensely blessed to hear the testimonies of my team members. After learning of their hardships, I found that I could easily relate to them. Since we made an agreement not to discuss the stories until all the members took their turns, I remained silent. As each day passed, my mind grew wild inside, itching to get everything off my chest.

On the sixth week, the very last week, my turn finally came. I was more than ready to share. Dinner that night didn't taste as good so I only took a few bites. After the team finished their meals and had the kitchen clean, my teammates sat down on one side of the wall while I sat on the other.

When the time approached, I began to read the first sentence in my writing. My hand shook ferociously, and my face flushed red while reading every word. My face was covered in tears by the time I got to the middle of the story, when I spoke about some of my biggest hardships. I was thankful to see that each word I spoke had an impact that was visible on the faces of my teammates. As the words traveled out of my mouth, I began to observe a sense of sorrow from them.

After finishing my story, many of my female teammates would approach me to hold a personal conversation with before we went to sleep. That night, the girls and I talked more about our lives and what we hoped to achieve. This was the trip that connected me to my teammates. Most importantly, I was thankful to be placed in a team setting that treated me like family with genuine love and affection.

I will never forget the words of my team leader Jinnie towards the end of the trip.

"You were bright, joyful, and a passionate member."

This trip helped me to experience and learn, for the first

time in my life, how I could overcome my adversities.

At the end of my trip to Thailand, my heart was so emboldened to speak and I was grateful to do so as soon as our team arrived at Korea. Standing on stage for the first time with a mic, I shared our team's testimony about our trip to Thailand, on behalf of Jinnie, for the college students at a small Korean church.

Tour with sisters, Jinnie on left

TKT Testimony in Korea, 2010

Flying back to New York a week later, I was excited to begin my adventure as a student at the start of my second senior year. I gathered the courage to continue participating in class each week. I began to speak up even more by participating in every lecture, even during group discussions in CRU. I never ceased to participate, willingly sharing my thoughts in class about the assigned readings. I was willing to speak at every opportunity. I was so excited that I could freely express my insights and opinions. I finally became content with myself, allowing me to slowly be myself.

When I returned from Thailand, I also shared my testimony with a church team, New Heart Missions Church, which my dad, mom, and sister attended. I was joyful to see my dad finally become a devoted member. Surprisingly, they were also flying to Thailand to share their testimonies.

I eagerly discussed my experiences with them, invited over to my house. They were happy to listen as it gave them an idea of what to expect. I noticed the enthusiasm that popped onto their faces as I described my story. Sharing my testimony influenced the way they approached their mission's trip, which provided me with immense joy. For me, it was proof that I could make a difference.

Upon the team's return from the trip, I had decided to attend my parent's local church. I hoped to become more accepting of my parents and feel like a part of the family, just like I did at Thailand.

Once I started attending, I continued to hear,

"You are so cute,"

"You are so tiny,"

"You are so small."

No matter how great I felt from being a member of the church, hearing these comments still unnerved me. But I persevered in my faith without feeling anxious about my height. Although I still held some reservations about my small body and bald head, I tried my best to believe I was welcomed. This led me to slowly develop stronger bonds with the other members.

Just before leaving for church every Sunday morning, I would spend my time preparing an outer layer to mask my body. I desired to take extra steps to disguise my skinny frame. I would never wear a short-sleeve shirt, afraid to show my skinny arms.

Clapping my hands and singing during service, however, stirred a sense of power in me. This led me to share during bible study and pray aloud during prayer time. I would eagerly chat with the members during lunch fellowship. These church activities helped me get through college. They gave me a sense of belonging that countered the sense of discord generated by my college and social life. Thanks to their wisdom, I learned many important lessons that continue to affect me until this day.

Chapter 17
A New Trial

A line from a song by Steve Fry captured my mind, "Then in my rest, there comes a test…"

These words had given me significant meaning in my life, explaining the full picture of how I have overcome trials related to my brain. Just before my graduation in 2012, I thought something was weird with my memory. I began to search for a neurologist. Once I found one, he conducted several tests. The results of the MRI and EEG showed that I had a 20% chance of having a seizure if I did not rest well and continued to face intense stress.

My neurologist emphasized that I needed to exercise, avoid stress, and eat well to reduce any chance of a seizure. I was discouraged by the news. His recommendations meant that I would have to give up the many activities I had grown accustomed to. I hid these results from my parents.

A couple of weeks later, my dad caught me having a seizure. It was coincidentally my first seizure after the college graduation, and he immediately rushed me to the hospital. While the seizure eventually subsided, we met the neurologist together.

During the appointment, my dad, in the presence of the neurologist, ordered me to take the prescribed medications. I took the pills, trusting it would work, but the seizures worsened. My problems did not end there. I quickly developed rashes from the medication, and severe acne blemishes and rosacea over my face. My self-esteem was battered once again.

My mom broke down in tears, while my dad would gasp in surprise whenever he saw me. Even my sister became utterly shocked to the point that she immediately passed me skin cream. I was blown away by their concern for me. I could not believe that my sister cared enough to help me when we held strong barriers for a long time. I was shocked to see that my mom would offer me herbal supplements to help my immune system and maintain my body.

I had become so unaccustomed to this sort of care that I did not know how to respond. The herbal supplements that my mom gave me worked for a month. Even though I saw some improvements thanks to them, I was dissatisfied because my skin did not fully recover. Even a tiny scar from the pimple messed up my self-image as it was already so damaged. The constant thought, *People can easily see my scars and redness,* was wired in my head. When church service ended each week, I would rush out of the sanctuary to hide my face from the entire members. I only met those whom I served with weekly, and with whom I had bonded.

After a few weeks, I stopped using herbal supplements when it became clear that they were not working. At that point, I started to experiment with skin creams in hopes of fully healing my potholed face. But that developed blemishes even more. To prevent this problem from worsening, I carefully washed my face with a gentle cleanser, meticulously putting the skin products on my face. But I inevitably saw more pimples pop up on my face each morning.

Some of my friends sensed my extreme dismay and tried to comfort me; however, I could not accept it. I could never expect to see beauty staring back from my mirror. In my follow-up visits with the neurologist, he began to raise the medication's dosage with each report of a new seizure. Raising the medication dosage only led to more seizures. I speculated that most of these seizures were most likely attributable to malnutrition, rather than fatigue and stress.

The frequency of my partial-seizures within a six-month period eventually led to a diagnosis of epilepsy. At church, Pastor Paul noticed my unhappiness and shame. One day after service, he offered to talk with me over coffee. After intently listening to my life's struggles, he had discerned what I needed and referred me to a counseling center. I agreed since I knew counseling was a good way to overcome emotional wounds and weaknesses. He signed me up for the sessions at the counseling center.

It was not easy at first, considering my dad's strong opposition to counseling because of his views on pride, shame, and societal stigma. Through the help of the church members, I fell into the routine. The first few sessions with my counselor, Ellen, started off very well. She was a good listener and I poured out my heart's contents to her. I sat on the edge of my seat each week, staring at the table, waiting to hear her feedback.

This continued for a few months, but over time, I wanted to plot a potential route of departure from the sessions. After the main talk about my bitter rage towards my parents, especially my mom, there was nothing particularly helpful that happened. It was disconcerting to hear the same words at the end of each session every week.

"Let it go."

I wondered how I could "let it go" when I had been internally wounded for years, incessantly, by parents and obnoxious peers. Words were not enough. My mind was not ready to let things go when resentment had been stamped in me.

So many problems had distressed my soul for more than a decade, but nonetheless, I continued to meet with Ellen. It reassured Pastor Paul as well as my parents, who had invested a great deal of money to help me escape from the slightest bruise and trauma in the process of slow healing.

I remember when some of our church members were visiting my friend, Sarah at her house. I came across one of her books. After she let me borrow her book, I spent the following week reading it. Then I read it again two more times. *How to Be Yourself*, by Joyce Meyers, was more than just an inspirational book—it transformed my life. This book gave me a positive mindset and boosted my confidence. The author's words were so powerful and encouraging that I wanted to step out and do something.

I became so overjoyed with this newfound inspiration that I decided to share what I read with my counselor. Her very last words to me were,

"Do what you want to do!"

Upon hearing this, the thought of serving the less fortunate tugged at my heart. I became driven to serve those who had less than I did. After volunteering in multiple organizations and non-profits that dealt with issues such as homelessness, human trafficking, and patients living with HIV/AIDS, I grew significantly adventurous.

I knew that this stemmed from talking to people to encourage them, while sharing my hardships and adversities with them too. Communicating with people whom I sympathized and also empathized with helped me develop a strong sense of duty and purpose in life.

Chapter 18
Boldness Risen

I decided it was time I replaced my old wig, which was beginning to show its age. While I initially intended to get another partial wig, I changed my mind and chose a synthetic whole wig. It was my last year in college. Putting it on after waiting for delivery for three months, I thought I looked good. Many friends noticed a difference since my human hair quality and synthetic quality showed a great distinction but I did not mind. I wore them until graduation. I took countless pictures from the new look with many friends in school, in ceremonies, and during student teaching.

CRU Event with Christine & Esther, 2012

After much deliberation, I returned to wearing just a hat, reminiscent of my elementary school years. Later, I switched to using scarves to cover my head as a better and more fashionable alternative. They looked rather good on me and were much lighter than hats and wigs, so I enjoyed wearing them for a while.

One night at church, the members shared their blessings. I began walking around back and forth while others continued sharing their experiences at Pastor Paul's house. I was slightly anxious about sharing, but slowly, I decided to leave my comfort zone. Pastor Paul noticed me and called me at last.

"Jenn, I feel you wanted to say something. Is there something you wanted to share?"

It was as though floodgates in me had been opened. I was still at first, then took the courage to share.

"It's been so tough wearing a wig for over a decade."

I confessed about my discomfort in a wig and my yearning for freedom in a world that was oppressive for people who could not conform to this pattern too. Most importantly, I shared of a conviction I longed to carry. A conviction that will instigate growth in myself.

"I want to be bold."

Then I lifted my jittery arm, shaking to take off my bandana. For the first time, I showed off my baldness. To everyone in the room. They gave me a standing ovation. My heart, mind, and soul were never this relieved. I was thankful to Pastor Paul and the church.

I began embracing myself for who I am, embracing my boldness. I became increasingly comfortable taking my hat off in public. I started in restaurants and in the gym. I continued to unburden myself, relieved of the literal and figurative weight, and showed off my self-assurance.

The Weaker, The Stronger

Meanwhile, as this was going on, epilepsy continued to haunt me. I continued taking the prescribed medications, which only led to more breakouts and scars, with rosacea and new pimples visible every morning.

On top of all this, I continued to suffer from memory loss. Over time, my case became particularly dire, with my cognition slowing down dramatically. It became a fight to retain my memory and make sure I remained functional. I became accident-prone due to the weakened memory, and despite my best efforts, my forgetfulness eventually became much severe that after five minutes, there would be no memory of a single face, name, or interactions. Everyone began looking the same to me. When someone greeted me, I greeted them back as if I knew exactly who they were, even though I did not.

There was no instant recognition. I only slowly remembered who they were during the conversation that followed. However, more often than not, I would forget their names, unless I saw them more than once a week, and even then, I would forget what we did together unless I got to know them better. This all came together in a vicious, self-fulfilling prediction of height and beauty issues, further exacerbated by seizures and medicine that led back to more anxiety.

The memory loss made me socially awkward—again, interfering with my ability to become closer to my friends. I felt judged and rejected when I forgot about their lives or past memories since they must feel insulted—or so I thought. I held the thought my memory loss stressed them out, so they did not want to associate with me.

These constant seizures, coupled with my anxiety, made me feel weak and paralyzed. It even prevented me from trying anything new due to the intense overfatigue throughout my body. I couldn't even think of attending graduate school. I began losing hope I had obtained after such a long time. But I began to practice letting go and get involved with others, which helped keep me stave off the dark forces. I constantly reminded myself to stay strong—I easily could fall back into the same trap. This was not easy.

Seizures and memory loss had combined forces. They were doing a good job at discouraging me too. My forgetfulness caused me to develop the same image I had of myself before heading to Thailand. I was close to returning to square one, worrying about how I was viewed by others. But I woke up one day with a new fire burning inside of me, a new boldness that propelled me to embrace myself like never before. I knew that no matter what I was going through, I needed to put myself forward and not worry about what others thought of me.

Through the constant prayer, faith, belief, and positivity, a boldness appeared that encouraged me to share my story in public. In September 2014, I affirmed myself as bald to celebrate my recovery. I began doing many things to live up to this commitment. I built the courage to display my bald head on Facebook in April 2015 and use it as a Facebook profile. Then, I made my first ever YouTube video in 2017, titled "My Epilepsy Story."

I was able to find the courage to do this after watching others share their stories online. They described their personal experiences living with epilepsy. This gave me the aspiration to make one as well. More surprisingly, for the first time ever, I made a speech in public, and even sang, at a local library. It was at an event called Open Mic, where anyone could come and freely speak in front of a large audience. When I first heard about it, I knew that I needed to participate in this activity.

Open Mic, 2018

I spoke my heart out in front of the crowd, and proved it by singing it aloud to prove that I am "Big, Bold, Beautiful", *Big* in soul; *Bold* in any circumstance due to my solid character; *Beautiful* despite how I looked. I sang it out too from the song, Beautiful, by Christina Aguilera. My mind told me to believe who I am— Big, Bold, Beautiful. On my way home from the Open Mic, I realized that the person whom I needed to convince of my greatness above all else was myself.

Belief In Myself

Considering I could handle hard tasks, I started attending graduate school for social work. In the middle of attending Nyack College, I was invited to a Friday night prayer service at JHOP, or Justice House of Prayer and started going regularly. During prayer time, they would also sing and dance and express their feelings or offer encouragement to the members over the mic. Sitting against the wall, I took my time talking to God, pleading for healing. In the midst of crying out, something popped into my head that enlightened my heart.

Eager to offer these words to the members, I walked up to the front of the stage. I grabbed the mic and expressed my deep hardship in both dealing with school and fighting for my health, especially my healing in epilepsy. Yet I exclaimed I would continue to maintain an attitude of faith no matter what the circumstances. I would keep these words that suddenly popped into my head. Then, I declared aloud,

"I am seizure free! My neurons are restored!"

Hearing all this, the entire crowd applauded.

From then on, I said these words every night during my shower. I continued to have seizures at least once a month, but I still did my best to keep the faith. Even when I was hospitalized or rushed to the emergency room multiple times, I still shouted aloud,

BIG BOLD BEAUTIFUL

"I am seizure free, and memory loss is restored."

* * * * * * * * * *

Despite my best efforts, the partial-seizures slowly grow into grand-mal seizures. A friend and I were standing at a distance in church. Seconds later, he watched me literally fall backward. By God's grace, he immediately ran to pick me back up. My next door neighbor was walking home. She discovered my body caught in between the entry door and the main door, hanging there, with my hands held to the key stuck on the door. She ran to help me, making sure to have no one use my keys to invade my home.

One summer, I was walking by in front of a police station and fainted on the street. I had bruised my head pretty badly. When I woke up, I was confused as to why I was sitting on a bench in a police station. A policeman had rushed to my side as soon as he saw me collapse during his break. Then, he had waited with me until the ambulance arrived.

All these events happened between 2017 to 2018. My heart was full of gratitude after hearing all this. They were my life saviors.

No matter the odds, I continued fighting the seizures in this way. I learned that adopting a ketogenic diet and gaining muscle would help. So I adapted my diet accordingly and joined a gym. As a result, I gained ten pounds in a year. Eating more than ever, resting more than ever, and taking great supplements and protein powders to help me, I was confident that I would get better. I would walk to the gym wearing a tank top, without a care in the world about what others thought of me. Even my parents were surprised by the changes in both my upper and lower body.

I no longer had a fear of looking skinny and was confident in my appearance for my goal is to be free from epilepsy, to stand up, step out, and fulfill my dreams. Thanks to all my newfound confidence, I decided it was time I began pursuing my dreams. It was up to me to step up. After learning how to lead or take responsibility in any organization or band, I yearned to start one on my own. I asked people to join me on this endeavor.

Jessica Leclere agreed to join. She and I began singing songs of worship in Central Park. By singing in public, it felt a lot like my childhood singing with my mic toy. It didn't matter how loud or how long we sang, I was elated we could sing our hearts out. This was a good sign of things to come.

Chapter 19
My Loving Souls

I often questioned what inspired the "beautiful" part of my newfound identity as Big, Bold, and Beautiful." I believed it happened after attending TORCC NYC, a local church in the city. A member, Ashley, welcomed me and was the first to call me "Big Jenn" after I had told her to call me "Lil Jenn." I had been using the nickname *Lil Jenn* every time I met someone new, saying with a smile,

"Hi, my name is Jennifer, but you can call me "Lil Jenn.""

I modeled my nickname after the American singer Lil Mama. Inspired by her confidence to call herself "Lil" because her small stature, I chose to do the same. I initially rejected Ashley's "Big Jenn" with words of false humility. But Ashley insisted,

"No, you are Big Jenn!"

She even mentioned it to the church quite often, and from then on, the whole church called me "Big Jenn." I shyly denied at first, but later accepted it, making me genuinely feel "big" at heart. Overtime, I enjoyed hearing my new name whenever they called me.

TORCC made me feel special in essence. The members of the church would encourage me with loving words like,

"You are so beautiful."

"You have so many talents."

"You are so creative."

Their encouragements helped me be truly myself a four-year-old again during church service. I no longer merely clapped my hands to worship God—I also lifted my hands up high, jumped, sang, danced, shouted, and dropped to my knees to express my honor for Him. I no longer displayed my love for Him half-heartedly, but wholeheartedly and genuinely, brimming with a passionate spirit and zeal.

* * * * * * * * * *

Seeing all this positive change in me, my parents' attitude towards me also began to change. They began displaying their love and affection more openly.

I survived a coma for a day after a seizure. This came from a prescription drug overdose, or taking a medication prescribed in high doses by a doctor. My parents regretted taking me there since this local hospital never received good reviews.

After I was discharged, my parents finally allowed the chance to share my feelings. I released every single scar I had been carrying in my heart for all those years. I confessed my hurt angrily towards them about their actions and behavior, and exposed the difficulties in overcoming my life medically and socially. My mom started weeping. Watching her cry made me want to fall into tears but I did my best to remain strong. My mom and dad both asked for my forgiveness. Out of compassion, I forgave them. It didn't remain permanent after facing some of the similar challenges while living with them. But I did my best to stay forgiving.

Shortly after, my dad started to show his love by singing love songs to me. One day, when he was dropping me off at graduate school, he timidly sang,

"Sanghee, Sanghee, my girl Sanghee, beautiful Sanghee, my girl Sanghee."

Hearing him, I giggled inside. It was awkward at first, but I slowly accepted the connection with his fatherly love. He started singing more often, more comfortably, whenever he saw me—at home when my mom and sister was not around, while having breakfast together, and driving me to school. Since my dad and I were not really morning people, I would hear him sing nearly every morning as soon as I woke up. I cannot forget the day when he walked over to me while singing and suddenly shook his hips and danced, showering his love on me. He would kiss me on the cheeks, which then became a morning ritual. These demonstrations of his love helped heal the deep scars in my heart.

There is a memory that still touches me today. My dad called me from the living room to come to him. Instead, he walked over to my room when I had just woken up. I lumbered along beside him, half asleep. He looked at me for a long moment, and then with a gentle smile asked,

"Jenn, my daughter, why are you so beautiful?"

I was silent for a few seconds. His loving words were so touching that I really had to struggle to keep a single tear from dropping. Every spoken word, every letter, was like a precious stone to me, stirring joy in my heart and bringing a strong sense of serenity. For the first time in years, he encouraged to me feel beautiful. He boosted the desire to drop the need for constant validation that I so craved. I thought to myself, *If my dad loves me so much, how much more does God?*

We built a lot of confidence in each other and were able to speak more freely. My dad would approach me with arms open wide while I was sitting on the couch. Seated next to me, he would ask about various personal matters.

"Why did you decide to quit your job?"

"Was it enjoyable living out alone?"

After explaining my reasoning, I had been grateful he understood, agreed, and fully accepted my thoughts on the matter. Scared that he might get upset, I did not tell my parents at first that I had refused to go back to graduate school even after the break from epilepsy. I decided to speak to my mom on the phone in order to create distance between us in case she was going to express her opposition.

I was glad she did not argue or respond negatively. Later that morning when my mom left for church, my dad sang and danced jubilantly for me, holding his arms over his head to make a love sign. His funny daddy act showed he knew and accepted it all.

A little later when I was pouring a bowl of cereal in the kitchen, my dad propped his elbow on the kitchen table. He put his hand on the side of his face to show his love in the Korean manner. His open display of fatherly love continued to decrease my fear of him. I was comfortable being loved by him. I would joyfully ask him to go shopping or have our own father-daughter dinner together.

His love indirectly helped sustain my self-esteem as I had one less source of anxiety to worry about. During that season of my life, I finally believed I was living the life of a child, enjoying the time and feeling like a daddy's girl once again. I didn't experience a hint of fear or distress from him.

"Hey Sanghee!" he would shout smiling in the middle of watching television together.

"You didn't scare me," I say proudly.

"Yeah you were," he would say chuckling.

"Nope. My body didn't even flinch," I say sternly.

Dinner with Daddy, 2018

My mom was changing for the better as well. How I folded the laundry or tied the garbage bag when it was full no longer mattered to her. She never walked in to observe how thoroughly I vacuumed my own room. She was becoming more laid-back and less picky. I was more at ease around her because I felt like I could afford to be less than perfect. I was grateful to see that she was expressing what she saw was good in me.

Alone with her one afternoon on her day off, I wondered why the house was so quiet. My mom is always active at home especially in the kitchen. I walked into her bedroom and found her sick in bed. I held a good chat with her to help sustain her strength. Out of nowhere, my mom requested a task for her.

"Jenn, make me tofu stew," she answered softly.

I was exceedingly scared at first since it would be my first time making it in years. I had always refused to cook Korean stew to escape hearing even the smallest comments from my mom. Taking a big deep breath, I took the chance to make one. I wanted to help my mom regain her strength.

Just as I started to prepare, I was shocked to see my

mom in the kitchen. She wanted to cook with me. I was honored by her willingness to help when she wasn't well. Starting from scratch, she guided me as she took out the main ingredients: anchovies, tofu, and soybean paste. She explained the directions carefully in order to make it delicious. While chopping the vegetables, potatoes, and tofu, I did not hear a single preachy comment.

"You're doing well."

This was all I heard every time she walked over to observe. After half an hour, we had our first sip of the soup. It was amazing. Thanks to her help, I was eager to try it on my own. I recorded every ingredient and the directions in my journal. I cooked the tofu stew alone the week after.

Noticing her progress made minimizing stress and maintaining peace easier. She increasingly began to accept my mistakes, more so when I forgot to carry out her tasks. It kept my mind at ease, thus reducing my seizures. I also taught her a workout routine, which she was willing to learn. Teaching her some exercise moves, I felt proud as a daughter because she no longer underestimated me.

Taking up the role of a trainer to teach someone greatly improved my mood since I could spread to others what I had learned and tried for myself. I also began teaching my mom English so she would improve her skills. I felt free to correct her whenever she made a mistake.

"No No No! Not like this but like that!"

"Why didn't you listen?" I said speaking in the tone of an army commander. She would laugh and try again.

I never imagined I could allow this sort of authority in a joking manner. Eventually, we became close enough that she would come to my room each night to speak with me right before going to bed. She would often come to my room to ask how she would look in her outfit while attending church.

"Hey Jenn, come over here. How does my sleeve look?"

"Does the skirt look too long?"

"Jenn, can I borrow a scarf I can wear for church?"

I found it annoying at times but fun to spend a good short time with her, free to point out my opinions on it.

Her consistent hugs and random kisses on these occasions, like those of my dad, prompted a faster breakthrough for forgiveness and a sense of comfort in my heart. The conversations we had at these moments were also helpful. We often share our day at work and our personal issues, and discussing social or political concerns.

Her dedication to making a great breakfast meal each morning to benefit my health, despite her weaknesses in diabetes turned over my permanent view on her— a tiger mom into a gracious mother. Her sacrifice of time slowly altered my viewpoint on motherhood and shifted off the doubt of becoming a mother. All these changes came together to make me bolder than ever before.

To help my parents, I went on YouTube and using a cooking channel's help, I cooked chicken wings that were seasoned with vegetables and fried potatoes. That evening, I offered them to my parents. My dad took a few bites of each and mused,

"Hmm, this is pretty good. Honey, can you make yours like hers?" Facing my mom and asked.

My mom started cracking up while nodding her head.

"Because it tastes so much different from how you season it," he said after taking another bite.

Upon hearing this, my heart was elated. I was urging to make some more.

BIG BOLD BEAUTIFUL

Chapter 20
Big, Bold, Beautiful

I did my best to forget my face in order to believe I was beautiful, both inside and out. At first, I did not realize that advertisements on social media were there to remind me of how I should look. The severity of the seizures over time not only affected my memory and cognition, but also my body.

While growing up, I had no problem perspiring on my face while eating anything spicy. However, I broke out after eating anything remotely spicy. I would also sweat profusely. Even so, I chose to escape this by changing my attitude. It was a terrible challenge.

The side effects of the medication such as mood swings, anger, and insomnia even deceived me into falling into the trap of negativity. Through the constant practice of speaking out that I was beautiful and multi-talented, and with encouragement from friends, I maintained a positive mind to remain steadfast and self-controlled.

As I was once again going through a challenge, I was invited to an event at my church that centered on the topic of beauty called *Identify Her 2018*. We were asked to write on an index card issues that kept us from seeing ourselves as beautiful.

Candace—the leader of the event—without having read my index card, knew what the issues were that I had written down,

"Moles, rosacea, blemishes, and scars."

I was shocked! This gave me the motivation to get up in front of that large audience and share my insecurities. I didn't have to worry about anyone knowing because now everyone knew.

My skin problems did not matter anymore, and I began handling my own tasks, like seeking to recover my health, which is a priority. I was no longer concerned about handling any responsibility that demanded nearly all of my focus, time, and energy. I was motivated to live my life zealously.

Feeling big inside and out, I even made a tank top of my own that read "BIG JENN" across the front. I made other tanks with inspirational words. I was excited to wear all of them to the gym, using them to influence or motivate clients to grow strong, both mentally and physically. I have a strong desire to give them, as well as all those outside of the gym, the encouragement to sustain a *Never Give Up* attitude. At the same time, I was coming to terms with how I ought to behave in public.

At this point, I was also carefree about eating out in public or working out without my hat or scarf. People watched me as they entered and left places. But they, more often than not, smiled at me. They respected me for doing what I wanted to do and not being afraid of being judged because I was secure in my skin. I also decided to shave my entire head in order to donate my hair to the children in St. Jude's Children's hospital.

Jessica Lee, whom I had met long ago in middle school, offered to shave my head. This was the second time I was going bald and I decided to show it off in public, to reveal my bold spirit and show everyone how beautiful my head looked. This time, I posted my new look as my Facebook and Instagram profile pic.

Jessica Lee and Shaved Head, 2018

More Open to Speak

I also became more assertive in defending my identity.

People might identify me as small due to my surface image, but I did not keep silent about it. I had an active say in the matter. After bumping into a lady at a buffet restaurant, she said,

"I'm sorry—you go first, little one."

I immediately shot back,

"I'm not little, I'm big!"

Chuckling, she nodded and walked away.

I was walking down the street and noticed a big group of old, drunk, rowdy men approaching me in the opposite direction. As they passed me, they shouted,

"Hey cutie!"

Without a hint of fright, I replied, "Hey," raising my hand. They were impressed by my assertive attitude. I no longer shook when crossing the street, any street, even big ones with wide lanes. With a nice scarf on my head, pretty sunglasses on, and a small handbag slung over my shoulder, I crossed the street with my head held high, not once looking down.

When working with children at Kumon, a reading and math academy, the little ones always questioned my daily covering on my head or compare their height with mine.

"Why do you always wear that hat?"

"Because I love wearing a hat!" I answered happily.

"I am almost as tall as you!" they would smile widely.

"So what? Does that make you smarter than me?"

The students would always smile and then walk away.

There was a Kumon Family Night Event that my supervisor, Shalini Outram planned. With great snacks, activities, and games, it was an enjoyable night for both the children and parents. During the event, Dr. Outram announced for everyone to gather around for a story time led by myself. Since the summer, I yearned to share a storybook I wrote in my own words and with illustrations from my friends John J. Kim, Maria Tsang, and James Kim. The story was about adulthood. Thanks to Dr. Outram's approval, I was able to do so.

I started as soon as students sat down on the carpet, while I sat on a seat. I felt like a school teacher, reading the book in a classroom. Introducing the title, I started reading. I showed the pictures closely for the children to get a good grasp the illustration. I would even ask questions to help them navigate some knowledge of school around them in the future.

After finishing the story, I finally took off my hat to show everyone of my real looks— children, parents, and teachers included. I pointed out how we ought to view ourselves and especially others. I was proud to see the looks of inspiration for both the children and parents. A student hugged me as soon as it ended. It was a meaningful night.

* * * * * * * * * *

I was taking the bus to work and came across a bus driver I had met in high school. I shouted out,

"Hey! You're the bus driver who drove the Bayside route ten years ago! Are you still driving the same bus? I am Jennifer and I attended Bayside High School. I remember you drove a lot of students off to that school!"

"Hey, really? Oh, I think I do remember you. You stand out because you are petite."

From then on, we had conversations in front of the bus, even though it isn't common for passengers to speak with the bus driver. I would often randomly see him on the bus and we would greet each other and talk. It didn't matter who was listening, I freely spoke as I could. I was aware the passengers knew Jack and I recognized each other and bonded well. These interactions showed me I could consistently have conversations in public, confirming fear could be cast out, no longer having a hold on me.

Speaking of fear, I have become freer to share my thoughts to friends and family, especially my parents. After having been able to listen to each other's perspectives on serious matters, my parents and I are learning how to listen and respect each other's perspectives. I am so grateful for the changes that now allow me to joke around with my parents and finally feel more comfortable being myself around them. I gave my mom advice on how to eat healthier as a diabetic.

"Mom, is that chocolate?"

"No, almond dark chocolate. Someone gave it to me."

"Oh, I see. But be careful because I hear dark chocolate can be considered regular chocolate. The higher the percentage the better. You know what's best? Cacao! That has more quality than the highest percentage of dark chocolate. That's what I use in my yogurt."

For a moment, she chuckled and said,

"I agree with your dad when he says this all the time, 'there's nothing you don't know.'"

I would laugh and reply back,

"It's from research in books and the internet mom!"
Whenever my dad came home from work as an exterminator, he sought to hug me many times with his pesticide spray stained on his t-shirt. I would back off yelling like a little child, "no!" giving the reason to avoid getting his stains rubbed onto my pajamas. Chucking, he would yell back,

"Good for you!"

Fellowship with friends has been great as we get to share our daily lives, keeping in touch as we reveal our troubles and personal feelings with each other. Given the chance to sit down one on one at a cafe, or even in a group of five at church, I would confess my part. It has been a blessing to listen to their story and provide uplifting words by including similar circumstances I had encountered and overcome many times. I was never aware of it myself and would hear this from many.

"Jenn, you are such an encourager, a woman of faith and encouragement."

It has been quite heartening to hear when my greatest desire has always been to provide care and kindness out of sympathy as well as empathy of the hardships they were facing. Then, they may conquer the deep pain living inside of them.

I have become proactive and take the initiative whenever I can. When all the surroundings tell me I am worthless, I refuse to believe it. *A group doesn't join me? I'll join them! I asked someone to grab dinner with me but can't make it? She must be very busy or tired. I guess I'll wait, which is the hardest..*

I often posted performances of myself singing and dancing on Instagram and Facebook. I sang my emotions out, no longer hiding them. Whenever I go out with a team to share the gospel, I would take off my hat and sing aloud to encourage unbelievers to come to faith. Being confident in my vulnerability enabled me to reach larger audiences. This has helped to spread His Word far greater than before.

I also granted myself the desire to dance in public. Jessica Leclere and I initiated a public performance. We joyfully danced outside in the park, with my beautiful head displayed.

Practice at Ripley Studio, 2018

Now, I often post videos of myself while I am working out. However, my main focus remains to show videos of my love of singing while playing my junior guitar. My heart drives to showcase my skills to the world, alongside the joy in what I do as an average woman since I cannot play a regular guitar with my tiny hands.

* * * * * * * * * *

I was invited to a high school alumni's reunion and decided to join. After the arrival, I realized I had never met so many attendees since I had graduated earlier. I never had a chance to know most of them in school. Still, my heart was instantly filled with the desire to uplift the atmosphere.

As they continued to share gossip and drink, I gave a shout-out to all thirty alumni, grabbing their attention. As usual, I took off my hoodie and sang out loud,

"This little light of mine, I'm gonna let it shine. Bayside alumni, I'm so glad you are here, I'll miss you, I'll miss you, I'll miss you, all of you!"

They all smiled and cheered at this spectacle, which propelled my further on my quest to be…me.

Chapter 21
My Heart Now

It is not uncommon for a five-year-old, proud child to become a humble but confident young lady. However, it is uncommon for someone like me to achieve such a transformation, someone who had so many obstacles tossed her way simply because of *who* I was. But those obstacles molded me into the true person I am. It took years to believe there was something special about me. Loving people, including my parents, taught me I was worthy of being *big*. They taught me how to accept *beauty*. They gave me a model of how to stay *bold*.

I certainly do not know where my life would have led without a deadly, malignant incident and ongoing trials. Maybe I would have become a cocky, conceited, arrogant child who would grow up to become a mess of a woman. I could have been tormented permanently, living outside on the streets, mentally ill, as if my life had ended. Or, attention-starved, I might have become a prostitute, perhaps, enslaved to sexual labor.

However, because of everything that I had to overcome, I no longer feel small in my heart. I am no longer as timid, nor do I feel worthless or hopeless, as if someone had stolen something precious in me. I am confident in my own skin, regardless of what it looks like. Even now, I continue to work on and improve myself. Friends see my character clearly, noticing the turnaround in me.

There was much suffering throughout my life, which is

to be expected as,

I am not God. Life is not perfect, I thought to myself endlessly, *but if it were perfect, how could we endure when we encounter a single challenge? How can we help others when they are suffering? Isn't it easier to empathize with them and help them overcome because of the obstacles we faced?*

* * * * * * * * * *

Battlefield with epilepsy is painful, but it has opened up opportunities for love to grow within my home. Illness has brought my parents together, demonstrating their love for me. This has alleviated a lot of the weight on my shoulders. It has helped me look at my parents differently, no longer viewing them as authoritarian but instead as truly loving parents. I may have lost all those years of my innocent childhood when I was distanced by them, but now I feel like I am being compensated for my loss with their love and affection.

Meanwhile, life goes on. I continue to fight epilepsy and continue to work towards my recovery. I have written my experiences in my journal to encourage those who are enduring the same things that I have— children with cancer, living with social challenges, and affected by family dysfunction all around the world.

I give a desire to boost the mood of patients, young or old, who are struggling with epilepsy. I have been currently doing this by supporting the Epilepsy Foundation. I plan to visit the foundation and all the young patients one day to share my story and encourage them to the very best.

I seek to instill faith in their hearts and minds that all things are possible through the help of loved ones and oneself. Remember that all people are beautiful. No one is perfect, yet they are beautiful in many ways: not only big in presence but big in soul. Just like the way I maintained my unique identity as an individual, I reflect deeply, hoping for others to feel the same. Above all, I will never give up even in the deepest tribulation. I will keep my heart, mind, and attitude on solid ground.

Over the course of my life, the diagnosis transformed me. I have become humble, steadfast in love, and trustworthy. These key characteristics of my life helped me to grow and maintain maturity in my life.